Deprivation and the Infant School

A report of the work of the
Schools Council Research and Development Project
in Compensatory Education
(Department of Education, University College of Swansea)

Edited by
Maurice Chazan and Phillip Williams

1978
Published for the Schools Council
by
BASIL BLACKWELL OXFORD

British Library Cataloguing in Publication Data

Schools Council Research and Development
  Project in Compensatory Education
  Deprivation and the infant school.
    1. Schools Council Research and Develop-
  ment Project in Compensatory Education
      I. Title 2. Chazan, Maurice 3. Wil-
  liams, Philip
  371.9′67   LC4096.G7
  ISBN 0–631–18760–X

Typeset by Richard Clay (The Chaucer Press) Ltd,
Bungay, Suffolk
Printed in Great Britain by
Billing and Sons Ltd,
London, Guildford and Worcester

3-25 S M 6430

JVD JGR
(cha)

Deprivation and the Infant School

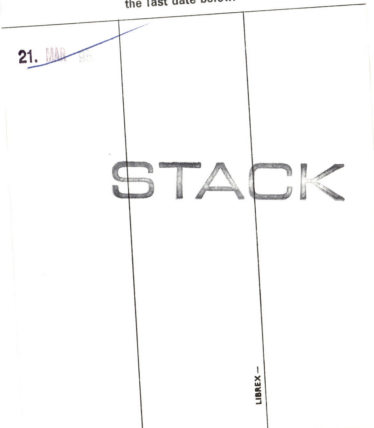
827466

Contents

v

Preface

From November 1967 until September 1972 a Research and Development Project in Compensatory Education, supported by the Schools Council, was based in the Department of Education of the University College of Swansea. The project, which was concerned with children of infant school age in selected areas in England and Wales, had three main aims:

1. to provide screening techniques so that children in need of compensatory education might be identified as soon as possible after school entry;
2. to make longitudinal studies of infant school children in 'deprived areas', with particular reference to their response to schooling and their emotional development;
3. to develop language materials which might be used to help culturally deprived children at the infant school stage.

Arising out of the work of the project team, a number of books and articles have been published, in addition to screening techniques and a handbook for infant school teachers containing suggestions for fostering language development. In view of the wide scope of the project's output, and since some of the research reports are necessarily detailed and technical, it was felt by the Schools Council that a publication summarizing the work of the project as a whole would prove useful. The members of the research team readily acceded to a request from the Schools Council to prepare such a book, and, in this volume, have attempted to present the main findings of the investigations carried out by the project, indicating, wherever possible, the implications of these findings for classroom practice.

Although the project was concerned with the infant school period, it seemed of value, at the outset, to investigate what effect material and cultural deprivation might have had on the children who made up the project sample, *before* they entered the infant school. Accordingly, a selected sample of the children who were living in 'deprived areas' was compared with a control group of children who were living in relatively advantaged localities in regard to:

1. the extent to which the parents were providing experiences which might be considered as helpful to the children in their subsequent adjustment to school;
2. the extent to which the children were showing behavioural disturbance of different types in their mothers' view, before going to the infant school.

The findings of this study (involving 122 children) are reported in 'Just Before School' (Chazan, Laing and Jackson, 1971) and are not discussed in this volume.

Throughout this book, the writers have tried to use technical terms as little as possible and to avoid lengthy discussions of statistical procedures. In order to keep the book short, basic tables and descriptions of tests involved have been omitted. However, full information on the research design, methods of assessment and statistical approaches used in the investigations described will be found in the main reports of the project (see References, p. 119 foll.) and it is hoped that the interested reader will refer to these as appropriate.

The work of the project was possible only with the full co-operation of the children involved, their parents and teachers, and many other people. To all who helped in this work, as well as to the Schools Council, the members of the research team would like to express their gratitude.

M.C.
P.W.

I

Introduction

In recent years there has been a growing concern for children whose educational progress is impeded by environmental handicaps such as poverty, membership of a minority group, or a background offering little emotional stability or cultural stimulation. On the premise that the handicaps of these children, usually referred to as 'deprived' or 'socially disadvantaged', can be removed or remedied by social and educational action, compensatory programmes on a wide scale have been put into operation in the United States of America, designed to improve education from the pre-school to the high-school level (Little and Smith, 1971).

In this country, although both research studies and official reports have highlighted the adverse effects of an unfavourable home background on a child's progress at school (see Chazan, 1973), action to help disadvantaged children has been more limited. However, money has been allocated by the government for improving old and inadequate school buildings and for giving an extra allowance to teachers in schools designated as facing exceptional difficulties. In addition to local authorities' own efforts, there has been a national Urban Aid programme, concentrating on the provision of new nursery classes and schools and on improving the social services in areas of greatest need. In a number of areas, Community Development Programmes, which include among their aims help for the deprived section of the community, have been developed. In a variety of ways, schools have been giving special help to pupils considered to be educationally handicapped because of social disadvantage. To help in the dissemination of knowledge of ways of combating disadvantage, an independent national Centre for Information and Advice on Educational Disadvantage, based in Manchester, was established in 1975 by the Secretary of State for Education and Science.

It has been acknowledged that, in spite of the voluminous American literature, much more needs to be known about the effects of deprivation on children in the context of social conditions in this country, and consequently a number of research projects have been established in recent years to study more precisely how deprivation affects children's development and school progress and to suggest possible remedies. At the pre-school level, an action-research project was started in 1968 by the National Foundation for Educational Research, with the aim of introducing and evaluating a compensatory programme for language and perceptual stimulation for disadvantaged children attending nursery schools (H. L. Williams, 1973; Woodhead, 1977).

In the same year, a wide-ranging Educational Priority Areas Project was set up by the Social Science Research Council in conjunction with the Department of Education and Science, to experiment with various forms of action to help deprived children and to make recommendations for appropriate educational and social policy (Halsey, 1972; Morrison, 1974; Payne, 1974; Barnes, 1975; Smith, 1975). In November 1967, the Schools Council, which had previously set up a working party to consider the problems of secondary school children suffering from social handicaps (Schools Council, 1970), established a Research and Development Project in Compensatory Education in the Department of Education of the University College of Swansea, which had the main aims of devising techniques to identify children 'at risk' at the infant school stage, studying the problems of deprived infant school children, and producing materials to help the language development of these children.

A CHILD-CENTRED APPROACH

The concept of 'educational priority areas' has tended to dominate thinking on the needs of deprived children in Britain, ever since the Plowden Report on primary education (1967) focussed attention on the need for 'positive discrimination' in favour of areas of greatest need—those characterized by a high incidence of poverty, large families, bad housing conditions, absenteeism and truancy from school and broken homes. The identification of such areas is indeed a useful starting-point in the redistribution of resources which is needed to bring extra help to families suffering from social and economic disadvantages. On the basis of action-research in England, Halsey (1972) concluded that the educational priority area, despite its difficulties of definition, is a socially and administratively viable unit through which to apply the principle of positive discrimination. However, Halsey was careful to point out that while a focus on locality is important, 'in the end,

2

the appropriate unit is the individual and his family'.

Although concerned with the problems of schools in areas that could be considered deprived in a number of respects, the Schools Council Project in Compensatory Education, whose work is discussed in this book, adopted a predominantly child-centred approach, putting the emphasis on the needs of the individual child. It is stressed that there is no clear-cut, homogeneous category of children who can be labelled as 'deprived' or 'disadvantaged', or who have very definite or specific characteristics which are invariably associated with conditions of deprivation. Research into the causes of school failure has repeatedly highlighted the importance of psychological as well as material factors in the home, although psychological and material factors are usually interrelated to some extent. Children may be deprived in a variety of ways, and in assessing the effects of deprivation on children, many variables have to be taken into account. The work of the project showed that many children in deprived areas enter school reasonably or even very well equipped to cope with the demands of school, and that a number of children not considered to be deprived perform as badly as very deprived school entrants (see Ferguson *et al.*, 1971 for a discussion of the inadequacy of an area or school-based approach to the problem of identifying children 'at risk').

Consonant with the emphasis on the individual child and his family, the project, while recognizing the usefulness of broad categorizations in terms of measures of 'social class', has stressed the need to make studies *within* as well as *between* social class groupings, and some of the work undertaken aimed at highlighting variations within deprived areas. The project, therefore, would endorse the view of Halsey (1972) that '... the use of the district as a means of identifying problems and allocating resources is ... no more than a convenient framework within which closer and more detailed work has to be done with schools, school classes, individuals and families in order to realize a fully effective policy of positive discrimination' (p. 181).

ORGANIZATION AND SCOPE OF PROJECT

To carry out the three main aims previously mentioned, the project was organized into four units: (i) the Identification Techniques Unit; (ii) the Unit for the Study of Emotional Development and Response

3

to Schooling; (iii) the Programme Development Unit; and (iv) the Welsh Language Unit.

(i) *Identification Techniques Unit*

This unit aimed at providing simple screening techniques to facilitate early identification of children in need of special help at the infant school stage. For this purpose, the unit has produced the Swansea Evaluation Profile for School Entrants (Evans *et al.*, 1978). The development of the Profile, involving a sample of nearly 700 children is described by Roy Evans in Chapter 2 of this volume.

(ii) *The Unit for the Study of Emotional Development and Response to Schooling*

The main aims of this unit were as follows:

to examine the effects of material and cultural deprivation on the educational, social and emotional development of infant school children;

to study the aims, methods and facilities of, and problems facing, a sample of schools serving children from 'deprived' backgrounds, and to compare these problems with those met within schools serving children from 'settled working-class' and 'middle-class' backgrounds; and

to liaise with the Programme Development Unit in the development of compensatory language materials based on the information gained from these studies and from discussions with teachers.

General survey. In order to study the association between deprivation and children's progress and adjustment in school at various stages during the infant school period, a broad survey of a sample of infant school children (involving 26 schools and, initially, 690 children) in urban areas over a three-year period was undertaken by the above unit (the sample was different from that involved in the work of the Identification Techniques Unit). In addition to obtaining information about the progress of the children, investigations were carried out into the views of headteachers and class teachers on the problems they

4

faced arising out of deprivation, as well as on approaches to teaching in the infant school, contact between home and school and the use of social and allied services. Also, a sample of 120 parents, representing a cross-section of parents of children drawn from the main sample, was interviewed concerning their use of services and links with schools.

Rural study. Although the emphasis of most studies of deprived children has been on problems arising from urban conditions, deprivation is not, of course, limited to urban areas. Teachers often feel that children from remote country areas start school with certain disadvantages, although these may be of a different kind from those associated with urban deprivation. It was, therefore, decided to study a small sample of children (62 children in 11 infant schools) in one rural county. Much of the school-based information sought was identical with that requested in the urban areas, and, additionally, the homes of all the children were visited to obtain data on their family background.

Intensive studies. In addition to the general survey, the unit team felt that it was important to make studies in depth of children living in deprived areas, which would involve them in close contact with the children, as well as with the parents and teachers. Since little work has been carried out to show the effects of different levels of cultural and material deprivation on children's development *within* deprived areas, the two intensive studies carried out were both concerned with comparisons between groups of children all living in deprived urban areas.

The first study (referred to in the following chapters as *Intensive Study A*) compared two groups of children (52 pairs), matched for age, sex, school and non-verbal intelligence but differentiated with respect to home background, one group being rated as highly deprived culturally and materially, the other as relatively advantaged. Since research to date has indicated that disadvantaged children show particular limitations in their linguistic and conceptual development when compared with children from more advantageous home backgrounds, this study was focussed mainly, though not solely, on these aspects of development.

The second study (to be referred to as *Intensive Study B*) was concerned with a group of children, who, in their teachers' estimate, presented marked problems of emotional and social adjustment during

5

their first year in the infant school. As such problems often affect educational achievement, the main aims of this enquiry were to ascertain the extent and persistence of the difficulties, their relationship with variables in the home background, and the nature of the help and guidance needed by these children and their families. The problems presented by this group (containing 39 children) were highlighted by comparison with a control group of 42 children living in similar areas but picked out as being particularly well adjusted in school.

The work of the Unit for the Study of Emotional Development and Response to Schooling is fully reported in 'Studies of Infant School Children'—Volumes I, 'Deprivation and School Progress' (Chazan, Laing, Cox, Jackson and Lloyd, 1976), and II, 'Deprivation and Development' (Chazan, Cox, Jackson and Laing, 1977). In the present volume the findings of the enquiries carried out are discussed in Chapter 3, where Alice Laing reviews the educational progress of the children; in Chapter 4, in which Maurice Chazan considers aspects of social adjustment; in Chapter 5, where language skills are discussed by Theo Cox; and in Chapter 8, in which Susan Jackson writes about the involvement of the parents in their children's education.

(iii) *Programme Development Unit*

The aim of this unit was to devise materials which might be of use to teachers in the work with deprived children. In view of the evidence indicating that these children tend to show considerable deficits in language development, the unit focussed its attention on this area, and devoted its resources to producing a handbook for teachers containing suggestions for fostering language development mainly in the first years of the infant school (Language Development and the Disadvantaged Child, Downes, 1978). The approaches adopted in producing the handbook are discussed in Chapter 6 by Theo Cox and Galen Downes.

(iv) *Welsh Language Unit*

This unit was established in order to study the effects of material and cultural deprivation upon the linguistic development, adjustment to

6

the school situation and educational attainments of Welsh-speaking infant school children. Although there are relatively few highly deprived children in the Welsh-speaking areas of Wales, these children face particular difficulties in having to cope with two languages during their period in the infant school, and it was considered desirable to attempt to throw some light on the nature and extent of these difficulties. A matched group design, involving 32 pairs of children, was adopted, similar to that used in Intensive Study A described above. The study is summarized by Gwyneth Lloyd in Chapter 7.

CONCLUSION

The Schools Council Research and Development Project was undertaken because it was felt that we need to know much more about the identification, school progress and adjustment of children living in conditions of deprivation, as well as about ways of helping them. It has been said of compensatory programmes that they 'cannot compensate for society' (Bernstein, 1970) and that they are 'a lost cause' (Eysenck, 1969). While it is true that the concept of deprivation needs careful examination and that compensatory programmes should be evaluated as rigorously as possible, such judgements overstate the case against compensatory education. While educational measures alone cannot solve problems arising from deprivation, they can help to solve these problems; and too little has been done in the way of compensatory education in this country for any firm conclusions to be drawn about its efficacy. It is hoped that the work carried out by the project and described in this book will help to promote a better understanding of the nature of educational handicap, and lead to appropriate educational and social action being taken to help children at risk.

2

The Identification of Children 'at risk' of Educational Handicap

As previously stated, one of the main aims of the Schools Council Project in Compensatory Education was to develop suitable screening procedures for identifying those entrants to infant schools who are in need of compensatory education. The purpose of this chapter is to describe the development of screening procedures which were produced in accordance with this aim.

The Swansea Evaluation Profile, as the screening procedures are called, was developed over a period of nearly five years and is the result of an intensive longitudinal study of nearly 700 children. The work could not have been completed without the active participation of many teachers, medical officers, health visitors and welfare officers, who carried out the main task of collecting information on the children's backgrounds and school progress, and of locating children whose families had moved during the study. This co-operation provided an essential means of exchanging ideas about the usefulness of assessment material in the infant classroom and the feasibility of obtaining specific items of information.

The development of these materials started from the assumption that the earlier children's educational needs can be identified, the greater is the chance for effective intervention. A number of procedures designed to screen school entrants had already been developed in the United States of America. Evans and Ferguson (1974) have surveyed these procedures and have indicated why there is a need for screening techniques to be developed in this country and for their effectiveness in identifying children's needs to be evaluated. It is not the purpose of this chapter to provide a detailed account of the screening instrument that emerged. This is given in the Technical Manual (Evans, 1978) which contains full details of the sample, of the pre-pilot and pilot phases, and of the analyses which led to the construction of these profiles.

It is fully realized that it is not possible to identify with complete accuracy those school entrants who will show specific problems at the

8

end of their infant school career: no procedure can do this. But the different groupings that the profile suggests, and the risk scores that it provides, will point to children over whose development special care needs to be taken. The results of screening should be used, not as fixed labels, but rather as warning signals, indicating which children need to be given the extra care that the 'at risk' signal suggests.

As stressed in the previous chapter, there is justification for a child-centred approach to the identification of need, and for assessing the 'educational risk' associated with each child. Three issues need to be tackled if compensatory education is to be effective at the primary school stage. These are:

(i) the identification and prediction at an early age of those children who are likely to need some form of special help;
(ii) the diagnosis of specific difficulties and needs in individual children;
(iii) the prescription of an effective programme of action.

The preventative aspect of compensatory education is possible only if the relevant risk factors have been highlighted and their individual and collective effects have been established. The rationale of the identification process is essentially to call the school's attention to the problem before the problem itself does, thereby permitting more successful intervention on behalf of the child.

PREDICTION OF EDUCATIONAL HANDICAP

In September 1968, the Identification Techniques Unit of the Schools Council Research and Development Project in Compensatory Education embarked on the first stage of a three year longitudinal study of a large group of five-year-old school entrants. The main aims of the study were stated as:

1. to provide simple screening techniques which would enable school entrants who were 'at risk' educationally to be identified as early as possible in their school careers;
2. to consider the production of an educational 'at risk' register;
3. to develop methods for assessing some educational and psycho-logical characteristics of children aged five to eight years. It was

9

also felt that the unit would make useful contributions to knowledge through

  (i) describing the medical, social and psychological characteristics of a population of children entering a judgement sample of twelve schools;
 (ii) providing information on the longitudinal development over the five- to eight-year-old range of some psychological and educational characteristics of a sample of the population;
(iii) identifying those medical, social and psychological characteristics of the population of five-year-old entrants which have most relevance to their educational performance at eight.

This chapter is mainly concerned with the first aim, i.e. with the development of screening techniques. The remaining aspects of the work of the unit are dealt with fully elsewhere. Ferguson (1972) describes the perceptual, motor and language skills of school entrants in deprived areas; and the psychological, medical and socio-cultural correlates of educational progress of children within the sample are discussed by Evans (1973). A test of phonic skills was developed in 1971 by Williams *et al.*, and Davies and Williams (1974) consider aspects of early reading growth.

The main study design

The Schools Council Field Report No. 6 (1968)* outlined the way in which the work was being organized. The full experimental design, including the pre-pilot and pilot stages of the investigation, is described by Evans (1978). Since the main experiment was basically concerned with prediction, the essential stages required by the design may be summarized as:

 (a) definition of the sample;
 (b) collection of initial information at school entry—approximately five years of age;
 (c) collection of educational progress data at the end of the infant school, i.e. at seven plus years of age;

* Now out of print.

(d) the analysis of the data to discover the meaningful relationships between the data collected at the two points in time;
(e) the compilation of the screening device itself on the basis of relationships which emerged during the analyses.

The sample

The Unit worked with children who entered the reception classes of twelve infant schools or departments between 2nd September 1968 and 1st September 1969, and who reached their fifth birthday within this period. Six of the infant schools were in the Midlands and six in South Wales. Of the six schools in each area, four were nominated as serving 'deprived' areas, one as serving a 'settled working-class' area, and one a suburban residential or 'advantaged' area. The nominations in each of these categories were made by the local education authorities concerned, in accordance with suggestions that the schools ideally should be:

(a) typical of their kind within the authority;
(b) routinely admitting about 60 children annually;
(c) without large numbers of immigrants.

The third restriction may appear somewhat unusual in view of the emphasis that has been put both in the United States and in this country on compensatory action for various non-white ethnic groups. Only a limited representation of immigrants was sought in the present study, not because the problems thrown up by these children were regarded as unimportant but because it was not the purpose of the study to examine the particular problems posed by them in the educational system. The investigation of the learning difficulties of such children was felt to be a matter of some urgency, but to require separate consideration.

It was expected at the outset that the judgement sample of twelve schools would provide a population of between 700 and 800 children for longitudinal study. However, since the sample was to be accumulated at regular intervals throughout the school year 1968 to 1969, its precise size and constitution could not be forecast at any stage prior to the point at which all the available information on each child had been recorded and collated. This was at the end of the school year,

11

i.e. August 1969. The expectation of sample size was in fact largely borne out, and by July 1969, 789 children had been admitted to the twelve schools.

The actual sample available to the study was, nevertheless, attenuated through the refusal of some parents to allow their children to co-operate and through the removal of some families to other areas. At the outset, therefore, 695 children were effectively available for study. Losses from the sample were, however, a continuing problem, and although efforts were made to trace many of the children who moved away from their original schools, inevitably these were not completely successful. In consequence, by the end of the three-year study, the sample had been reduced to 627 children, on whom relatively complete information was available at both points in time. It was this sample which provided the main focus group for the prediction study. For each of these children at school entry, information about their situation was gained in four main ways, described below.

Collection of initial data at school entry

(a) *Home background assessment.* This important area was rated by the headteacher on the basis of a structured interview with one parent, usually the mother. The main aspects of this assessment were the economic viability of the home, the cultural provision within the home, the material and physical circumstances of the family and the parents' attitude to and interest in the child's education. These interviews, wherever possible, formed part of the normal admission procedure, although, where necessary, headteachers arranged special interviews with the mother.

(b) *Medical assessment.* This was in two parts, one of which was conducted by the School Medical Officer and the other by the Health Visitor. The information gained by the Medical Officer was based on the standard school medical examination and produced a picture of the child's physical and medical status at the time of school entry. The information obtained by the Health Visitor was related to important developmental milestones from birth to school entry, and she also sought information on the presence or otherwise of difficulties in the pre-natal stage of development.

(c) *Individual assessment of children.* A battery of fourteen psychometric devices was developed to provide measures of the intellectual, linguistic, perceptual and motor development of the children being studied. These assessments were made by members of the research team within a few weeks of a child entering school. Because of the paucity of existing techniques for assessing school entrants on various aspects of cognitive functioning, many of these devices were constructed by the research team.

(d) *Teacher's assessment.* Class teachers were asked to provide information on each child in the school situation. The main areas of interest were the child's adjustment to the experience of school, his social development within the class and his educational potential. These assessments, too, were made a few weeks after school entry.

In general all the information collected at this stage of the enquiry was obtained in the school situation. In addition to the parents' interview with the headteacher, the medical examinations and the Health Visitors' questionnaire were also completed at the schools. In a few instances, however, it was necessary for an Education Welfare Officer to obtain some of the home background information and for a Health Visitor to visit the homes of those parents who were unable to attend the school at the time of their child's medical examination.

The emphasis on the school as the main agency for the collection of information was regarded as important *in principle*. The reason for this was that, since the study aimed at producing a screening device for use in the school situation, it was important that information which such a device ultimately requested should be routinely available within the school and related to the objectives of the school.

Final data collection at 7 +

Since the main study was essentially one of prediction, it was necessary that, in addition to the collection of information descriptive of the sample of children at school entry, the educational progress of all the children should be assessed at the end of their infant school careers. These latter assessments represented the criteria for prediction. During the intervening 2–3 years the children in the sample underwent a normal school routine and no experimental programmes were initiated by the research team.

During their last term at infant school two sets of measures were obtained for each child in the sample. These were:

(a) *School schedule.* The schedule was in two parts. Part 1 dealt with the nature of the educational provision available to each child at the time of assessment and requested factual information on school attendance, changes in family circumstances, possible referral to the educational psychologist or child guidance clinic and need for special treatment. The headteachers provided this information. Part 2 was completed by the class teacher, and was designed to obtain information on the child's overall progress at school, his standing in particular areas of the curriculum, and the patterns of behaviour and friendship he displayed. These data were based on rating scales and utilized the teacher's perceptions of her pupils' progress.

(b) *Psychometric criteria (attainment tests).* During the final stages of the project the research was mainly concerned with administering a battery of tests designed to measure the basic attainments of the children in the sample. The majority of tests in the battery were standardized tests, all of which are available through agencies in this country, together with a non-verbal measure of intellectual development. The main areas of development assessed were related to reading, number and vocabulary skills.

The analysis

The descriptive analysis of the population of children, both at the time of school entry and at the time of transfer to junior departments, has been described by Ferguson (1972) and Evans (1978). The problem of analysing the relationships between the two sets of data is one which requires the use of multivariate statistical techniques for its solution. A number of approaches are possible, by and large the most useful all being different forms of analysis of variance. The predictors which contribute most to the prediction can generally be separated out by formal tests of significance. In particular experimental conditions, each statistical method has its own advantages in the solution of the prediction problem, and each its own defects. Readers with psychometric interests may like to know that in the present study the form of analysis decided upon was as follows:

(1) Segmentation Analysis by criterion grouping, preceded by principal components analysis and exploratory regression analysis (Mode 1).

(2) Regression Analysis, preceded by principal components analysis, followed by an aggregation of significant predictors emerging from a series of linear analyses to form an additive scale. This 'risk' scale could be dichotomized into high or low risk categories through the selection of an appropriate cut-off point (Mode 2).

The first mode of analysis used as a criterion a broad measure of educational progress which was obtained from the battery of attainment tests used with the sample at 7 +. The analysis resulted in the division of the whole group of 627 children into a mutually exclusive series of sub-groups, each sub-group of children being completely specified by a unique combination of predictor categories, in such a way as to maximize the discrimination between them when related to the criterion. Not all the groups which emerged from the segmented population are of interest to the educationist who is concerned with identifying the need for compensatory education. The characteristics of many of the sub-groups indicated that their members had made normal school progress. It was useful to consider as part of the prediction scale only those predictors which characterized and defined those sub-groups of children for whom the general indications were underfunctioning or retarded development. These were to be regarded as 'high risk' sub-groups.

However, the result of limiting one's consideration to these special groups created a situation whereby, in a normal population, only a fraction of the children could, by definition, be so assigned. Taking a realistic view that a proportion of the population not classified as 'at risk' in this way would, nevertheless, exhibit educational handicaps later on in school, a measure of 'risk' for these children was obtained using the complementary procedure which emerged from the second mode of analysis. The final prediction scale contained the pertinent variables from both modes of analysis, and the 'risk' estimate would be made only if classification failed to apply. Either way the procedure would indicate those children for whom the prognosis was the likelihood of educational retardation in the absence of special intervention. The pattern of analysis finally adopted by this study is fully described by

15

Evans (1978), and so the strategy used in the analysis will not be given in full in this chapter. It is perhaps sufficient to note that, of the original 144 separate items of background and developmental data collected at the time the children entered school, only 13 were ultimately separated out from the analysis as making effective contributions to the prediction of educational risk. These are set out in Table 1.

Table 1

Most important predictors emerging from the analyses,
classified by schedule of origin

Schedule of Origin or *Area of Initial Enquiry*	*Description of Variable*
SECTION 1 *Sociocultural background* *(home background survey)*	1. Estimate of family's financial situation 2. Age father completed full-time education 3. Mother's further education after leaving school 4. Number of rooms occupied by family 5. Size of family
SECTION 2 *Teacher assessments of* *school adjustment, etc.*	1. Teacher's estimate of child's likely future progress 2. Term of entry 3. Type of school 4. Rutter (1967) Child Scale B (Infants)
SECTION 3 *Child development*	1. Test of symbols reading 2. Visual perception test 3. English Picture Vocabulary Test (Brimer and Dunn, 1962) 4. Test of numeracy

An inspection of Table 1 will reveal that the predictors which emerged fall into one of three aspects of a child's development:

   (i) the home background against which his learning is taking place;

16

(ii) the extent of his learning and development so far;
(iii) the way in which he has adjusted to the experience of school.

The screening procedure utilized these 13 variables. It will be noted that information from the medical assessment did not appear in this set of predictors.

THE USE OF THE PROFILE

This has been developed for use with children at entry to infant school in the first term of the reception class. For practical purposes, the descriptive title 'Evaluation Profile for School Entrants' has been adopted for the screening material. The Profile, which consists of assessments of the three aspects of a child's development listed above, brought together in the form of a record book, can be used in at least five ways.

1. *To give a picture of the new entrant to school*

The answers to the questions in the three sections of the record book help to give a picture of a new entrant to school. The information can be used to provide insight into the way children respond to the experience of school.

2. *To identify groups of children 'at risk'*

The screening procedure defines several groups of children who are likely to do poorly at the end of the infant school, and identifies them by using different combinations of items. The procedure also defines a group of children who are on the whole somewhat above average in ability and attainment, but who, nevertheless, are likely to show a deterioration in their school work owing to emotional or social problems.

There are four special care groups that are of particular interest when we are concerned with the identification of children 'at risk' of educational handicap. These will be described briefly below.

17

Group A The children allocated to this group were from families whose financial position was precarious, and who were either just managing or were suffering actual hardship. In addition, these children performed extremely poorly on the test of symbols reading and were, in their teachers' opinion, of average and below average ability. The group was the largest of the four special care groups identified, and 95 of the 627 children in the main sample fell into it at the end of their infant school career. This group of children had the lowest average performance of any of the eleven groups which the analysis isolated. It is important to note that the group's average score on a measure of non-verbal ability at this time was also the lowest of the groups, as was the average socio-economic status of the group. Children in this group tended to be very slow starters educationally.

Group B All children allocated to this group were from schools serving poor neighbourhoods, and from families whose fathers received no full-time school education beyond the age of about 14 years. In the opinion of their class teachers, these children were of average and below average ability, and their performance on the Symbols Test tended to reflect this view. It is important to note that there were no children in this group who performed *extremely* poorly on the test of symbols reading, and that the response pattern does allow children who perform extremely well on this test to be placed in this group.

Of the sample of 627 children studied, 38 were in this group. One of the interesting differences between groups A and B lies in their development at the start of infant schooling. The children of group A were slow starters and remained slow learners. The children of group B were not particularly weak developmentally at school entry, but, although their scores on the measures of vocabulary and language skills were not poor, they made a poor response to school. By the end of their infant schooling their standing on a broad measure of educational development was hardly better than that of group A.

Group C This is an interesting group in the sense that it is composed entirely of children whose progress through the infant school was predicted by their class teachers as likely to be 'above average' or 'exceptionally good'. As a group, however, their mean performance on the broad measures of educational attainment used in their last term at infant school was no better than that of children in group B.

However, the number of children who fell into this group was small, and the teacher will not normally meet many children of this kind. The greatest concentration of such children is likely to be found in schools in 'deprived' and 'settled workingclass' areas. Unlike group B or group A they seem to be intellectually able children whom their teachers felt showed promise at the time they entered school. Taken as a whole, there was a clear discrepancy between their performance and the teachers' expectations of them. There may be several explanations for this, but the evidence points towards underfunctioning as the most reasonable, and any child who satisfies the selection criteria for this group may require considerable help.

Group D Briefly, these were the children for whom the teachers' forecast was of an average, or below-average performance while at infant school, but whose results on a simple reading test indicated a potential which is certainly average and above. Furthermore, the children allocated to this group were not from schools serving 'deprived' areas. Their scores on the Rutter Child Scale indicated the existence of behavioural difficulties which in some cases were quite extreme. Sixty-nine of the sample of 627 children fell into this group. Unlike the other three groups, the children in it were not educationally weak at the end of their infant school careers. In fact, their performance was above the mean of the sample, as was their mean score on a non-verbal test of intellectual development. The group is included here since, in the main, their home circumstances led to an expectation of a good response to the infant school. However, there was a tendency for the group as a whole to deteriorate in relation to the rest of the sample, though it is not possible, without further verification, to indicate precisely the importance which can be attached to this tendency. It is noteworthy that this group contained a high proportion of relatively less stable children who needed careful handling.

It is not possible to describe the circumstances and achievements of the typical child of any group but case studies which underline some of the observed characteristics have been included in the Handbook (Evans *et al.*, 1978).

3. To provide an 'overall risk score'

The information collected can also be used to provide an overall risk score for those children who do not fit precisely into any one of the special groups defined in 2 above. The risk score provides an indication of the likelihood of a child having learning problems in school and the consequent need for some form of special care. Schools with a concentration of high-risk children among their intake may warrant special attention.

4. To provide an individual profile

A standard profile has been developed for comparison purposes, based on the mean scores obtained by the sample of 627 children on each section of the record book. To gain additional insight into the needs of those children identified as 'at risk', individual profiles may be drawn which, when referred to this standard profile, point out specific areas of deficit which carry implications for the children's later school progress. Once the areas of deficit have been established, the information may be used in two main ways:

(i) to make a decision regarding the suitability of 'special' as distinct from 'compensatory' education, in any given instance— the distinction suggested here is between poor development in a good environment and development in an adverse environment;

(ii) as a basis for educational or social action.

In the first case the distinction between 'special' and 'compensatory' education is not an easy one to make and, in certain circumstances, may be trivial from an operational standpoint. Nevertheless, it is obviously important for a teacher to know whether a child is achieving badly, in spite of favourable home and school circumstances, or whether adverse and inhibiting forces are operative in the child's environment, thus creating a basis for under-achievement and subsequent educational deterioration. In the former case, the child would appear to be a likely candidate for special education later on, while in the latter case the use of suitable compensatory action is clearly called for.

In the second case, one needs to consider the child's developmental test performance in conjunction with scores obtained in the other two sections, so that an intuitive evaluation based on this information will reveal whether or not the child is

(a) likely to progress normally with no handicap evident and no physio-medical defects;
(b) likely to be a slow learner, but with no handicap evident from his socio-cultural background or general adjustment to school, and with no adverse medical conditions;
(c) a bright child whose attainments will ultimately begin to fall off, as a result of the continued operation of unfavourable circumstances, poor health and so on;
(d) a below-average child whose total situation is likely to produce a progressive decline in attainment.

Evaluations of this nature are essentially tentative and should be viewed as such. In certain cases, lines of action suggest themselves. Children with poor language development and restricted vocabulary may benefit from a specific language programme, such as that developed by the project and intended for the first year after school entry. In other cases, the special handicaps exhibited will need extra investigations from psychologist, social worker, medical officer or specialist teachers. In either event, the net result will be the same, a greater understanding and knowledge of the child. This knowledge should be translated by the teacher into classroom action.

5. To predict basic attainments

The information may be used for predicting future attainments in the basic subjects. A quantitative assessment of the 'at risk' child's future attainment can be obtained through the use of equations which have been generated for this purpose. These are described in Evans (1978).

CONCLUSION

The purpose of this chapter has been to describe, in general terms, a practical approach to the identification of children 'at risk'. Most of the technical detail has been omitted, and, in consequence, it has not been possible to do more than indicate the direction which the work has taken, in the hope that this will stimulate further interest in this important area of educational assessment.

The development of the Profile is based on the assumption that the earlier children's educational needs can be identified, the greater is the chance of effective intervention. It is fully realized that it is not possible to identify accurately all children who will show specific problems when near the end of their stay in the infant school. But the different groups that the Profile suggests, and the risk scores that it provides, do point to children over whose development special care needs to be taken.

It is emphasized that the development of the Profile has not proceeded beyond what, in research terms, would be regarded as 'a period of experimentation'. It clearly needs extensive field trials, as the evidence relating to its validity is largely based on internal criteria. It is clearly of importance to assess the value of the Profile, whether in terms of its efficiency as a predictor or of its general usefulness, through further controlled studies with different samples of children in different schools. If such a study were undertaken, some changes in the present format or content could well be recommended, although some changes have already been incorporated into the Profile as a result of field trials with an early experimental version.

3

Educational Progress

This chapter is concerned with the educational progress of the urban and rural children surveyed by the Unit for the Study of Emotional Development and Response to Schooling (see Chapter 1 'Deprivation and School Progress', Chazan *et al.*, 1976). It should be borne in mind that no special measures were introduced for these children, whose progress was charted in the context of a normal three-year infant school programme. In view of the dearth of information on the effects of deprivation on children at the infant school stage in this country, it was felt that a study of this kind would be helpful to teachers in considering what changes, if any, might be required in the traditional infant school approach, if all children at this stage are to be given an education appropriate to their needs.

THE CHILDREN

1. *The urban sample*

In Chapter 2 the procedure developed by the project team for identifying children who may be 'at risk' educationally has been discussed. As no such techniques existed when this study of infant school progress was begun, the children to be studied were selected on an area basis. Three local education authorities were each asked to select four of their schools which they considered to be serving 'deprived' catchment areas.

No precise criteria of deprivation were stipulated, but when the 1966 census data for the areas so chosen were examined, it was found that the selection was a reasonably valid one, a number of disadvantaging conditions being present, e.g. well over a third of the working male population was in the Registrar-General's social classes IV and V; there was considerable family mobility both within and out of the local authority area; the majority of the adults had not continued their education beyond the minimum requirement; few of the houses were owner-occupied and there was evidence of overcrowding in some instances. The census data, therefore confirmed that the twelve schools selected (which were not the twelve schools mentioned in Chapter 2) did contain children who were likely to be disadvantaged because of pressures and deprivations in their environment. A further two schools were added to the original twelve in order to counteract losses through family mobility or from local authority clearance policies. A total of 372 children was involved, all born between 1st September 1963 and 31st March 1964, and all entering their respective schools in September 1968. They were studied over the three years of their infant schooling, and it is interesting to note that during that period 25 per cent of them were, in fact, lost to the sample.

To make the study meaningful, the progress of the children from these 'deprived' areas had to be compared with that of children whose environment was rather more favourable. The same LEAs were, therefore, each asked to select a further four schools, two of these serving 'settled working-class' areas and two serving 'middle-class' areas. The children going to these schools could be combined to form a 'control' group for comparison purposes, or considered separately where appropriate. To the sample total, therefore, were added six 'settled working-class' (SWC) schools, containing 174 children, and six 'middle-class' (MC) schools, containing 143 children, a total 'control' group of 317 children in twelve different schools, all born within the time limits already stated and all, as with the 'deprived' group, entering a full three-year infant course in September, 1968.

A number of differences in the composition of the 'disadvantaged' and the 'control' groups soon became apparent. The children in the 'deprived area' group (referred to hereafter as the DA group) were members of larger families than the children in the 'control area' group (CA group); more of them were later born (i.e. the fourth, fifth or later child in the family); over twice as many of them, in comparison with the national average, qualified for free school meals; and, because of the family mobility already mentioned, they were more likely to change school. The DA group children were fractionally older on average than the CA group and had rather poorer attendance; they also had a higher incidence of medical defects and disabilities (including defects of hearing and vision), more of them had poor teeth and more were considered to have poor speech. In both the DA ('deprived' area) group and the CA ('control' area) group, over 90 per cent of the mothers had made some contact with the school prior to their child's

24

entry, but only about a quarter of the DA children's fathers had done so compared with just over half of the CA children's fathers.

Some differences were also found in the schools the children attended. Not as many of the teachers in the DA schools were infant trained and they had not been teaching for as long as the teachers in the CA schools. There appeared to be rather greater difficulty in appointing staff to the DA schools and supply teachers were seldom obtained and unwilling to stay for any length of time. On the other hand, the DA schools had a more favourable teacher/pupil ratio and smaller classes, the class numbers in the CA schools being just above the national average while those in the DA schools were just below it. Teacher mobility was not excessively high in the DA schools, even though some of the schools had a rather greater number of adverse features than the CA schools and the provision of materials was in general poorer. Eleven out of the fourteen DA schools had no tape recorder, for example, compared with six out of the twelve CA schools. It would, however, be true to say that greater differences in the schools' staffing and facilities existed between the three areas studied, as a result of different local authority policies, than between the DA schools and the CA schools as a whole. It would also be true to say that the differences in the schools the children went to were not so great as the differences in the home backgrounds from which they came.

2. *The rural sample*

Deprivation is frequently associated with areas of inner urban decay only. In selecting the urban sample, an attempt was made to include in it children from areas other than decaying town centres but whose environment was nevertheless unfavourable, for example children living on bleak housing estates or in high rise flats. But to be cut off from easy access to places of interest and to lack the companionship of other children of the same age could amount to a degree of isolation which might also be considered as a form of deprivation. Sixty-two rural children were therefore selected so that their progress and attainments could be studied. These children were in the same age range as the urban children and attended eleven schools (10 of them all-age primary schools) in a small Welsh county. All were English-speaking in a predominantly English-speaking environment.

The schools they went to varied in size, the roll in the smallest being 29 and in the largest 200. Four of them lay within urban districts, but all contained some pupils from isolated homes. Five of the schools had only one class for infants and one had two classes. Nine of the schools were built before 1914; four had no central heating; four had no staffroom; indoor sanitation was lacking in several and one had no flush toilets at all. Other schools, of course, were well provided with amenities and the recently built schools compared favourably with the best of the town schools.

Isolation certainly had an effect on both the schools and the children. The schools were compelled to become largely self-sufficient and young teachers were reluctant to stay for long in the more remote parts of the county. Before going to school, the children had been almost completely home-based, sheer distance depriving them of many of the experiences which town children would take for granted. Yet when they went to school they settled in remarkably quickly and no difference in progress was found between the children from the most isolated homes and the others. Small teaching groups, parental encouragement and the involvement of the schools and their staffs in the general life of the community were advantages which seemed particularly helpful to the children's ability to make steady, adequate progress.

EDUCATIONAL ATTAINMENTS

Perhaps the most direct way of indicating the response made to the infant school programme by the children is to look at their attainments at the end of their three years in the infant school. In their ninth school term, all the children remaining in the sample were given a number of standardized tests, namely:

1. *Burt Word Recognition Test* (a short, straightforward test of mechanical reading ability);
2. *Neale Analysis of Reading Ability* (a test of the accuracy and rate of the child's reading and his comprehension of what he has read; it gives a good coverage of progress in reading skills once the child has passed the initial stages of learning to read);
3. *Daniels and Diack Spelling Test* (a test of the child's ability to spell fairly regular phonic constructions, each word being given in an appropriate context);

26

4. *Vocabulary sub-test from the Wechsler Intelligence Scale for Children (WISC)* (a test of vocabulary development, standardized on American children aged 5 to 15 years);

5. *National Foundation for Educational/Research – Basic Mathematics Test* (a test designed to assess the grasp of mathematical concepts and skills in top year infants. When this test was used, it was still in an experimental version and information on the performance of large groups of children on it was not available);

6. *National Foundation for Educational Research—Picture Test A* (although not designated as a test of intelligence, the items used in this non-verbal test involve the use of reasoning and inference and the results from it could therefore be considered to indicate the child's potential for learning).

An extremely clear-cut pattern emerged from the test results. As far as the urban sample was concerned, on all of the tests the CA ('control' area) children were superior in performance to the DA ('deprived' area) children. Of the CA children, the 'middle class' area (MC) group did outstandingly well, very much above the performance of the other CA children (i.e. the 'settled working-class' area group) and the DA children. This result was probably predictable, as the MC children were likely to have had all the chances for success both before and after school entry. The SWC children, too, had higher average scores than the DA children on all the tests except for the Basic Mathematics one, but it should be noted that the scores of the SWC children were nearer those of the DA children than were the MC children's scores and that a degree of overlap existed between the SWC and DA samples.

The pattern of superior performance held over all the MC schools, except for one where the average scores were lower than the SWC average scores and comparable with the DA scores. The DA schools showed greater variation in performance; for example, one was consistently higher on average than all the rest and neared the MC schools' scores, one was very like the SWC schools in performance and one showed very low average scores on the tests of reading, mathematics and 'intelligence'. The greatest variations in average scores were on the reading and spelling tests, perhaps because of the tests used but probably because of differences between schools in the emphasis placed on these skills.

When the results of the attainment tests were converted into achievement 'ages', it appeared that the MC children were performing on all the tests at a level which was six months to one year above their average chronological age. The SWC children were closer to their chronological age, being one month to six months above it in performance on all tests except Spelling. However, the DA children were one month to eleven months below their average chronological age on the tests (except for the rate score on the Neale Analysis of Reading, an aspect of the test which did not seem particularly reliable at this age).

On the Burt Word Recognition Test, there were roughly twice as many DA children with reading ages below 7 years as CA children. A reading age of 6 years or less being taken to indicate retardation (i.e. eighteen months or more below the average chronological age of the sample), it was found that thirty-eight per cent of the DA group, as compared with twelve per cent of the CA group, could be classified as retarded. Retardation in spelling, using the same criterion, showed a very similar result, with thirty-three per cent of the DA children and eight per cent of the CA children recording a spelling age of 6 years or less. Yet on the non-verbal 'intelligence' test, there was not a preponderance of low scorers among the DA children, although the proportion of low scorers was higher in the DA group than in either of the 'control' groups (MC or SWC). Of the DA children with reading ages on the Burt Word Recognition Test of 5 years or less, a serious degree of retardation, thirty-six per cent had average or above average 'intelligence' test scores. It would seem, therefore, that in a number of cases, retardation was not associated with poor intellectual endowment but could be thought of as an indication of considerable under-functioning.

What of the performance of the rural children? On the Mathematics test and the Picture Test A, the average performance of the rural area (RA) group was superior to that of the urban sample as a whole, but in all other tests, no real differences in performance existed. When the urban sample was broken down into its various components, it appeared that the level of performance of the RA children was consistently lower than that of the MC children, although only fractionally so in the two tests mentioned above, and was, in a number of instances, similar to that of the SWC group.

The results of the various groups on the Picture Test A call for further examination, as the poorer average performance of the DA children on this test, in comparison with the other children, might be related in an important way to their lower level of attainment. When this was examined statistically, it was found that, although the effect of 'intelligence' (as estimated by Picture Test A) on attainment was indeed powerful, so, to a lesser extent, as far as the urban children were concerned, was the effect of the type of area from which the school drew its pupils. In other words, while intelligence made a considerable contribution to the level of attainment reached by the DA children at the end of their infant schooling, the factors in their home background which differentiated them from their more favoured peers also played their part. This was not the case in the rural sample. The children who came from the RA homes which were rated as 'most deprived' relative to the others in the RA group had the lowest scores on every test, markedly so in some cases. But these results seemed to be linked only to the 'intelligence' measure. The extent of deprivation in the home had by itself little effect on performance. It must be remembered, of course, that none of the homes in the RA sample was as deprived, materially or culturally, as some of those in the urban sample.

It is not easy to disentangle the contribution which limited intellectual endowment and deprivation make separately to educational progress and it is anyway rather a dubious undertaking to attempt to do so. Just as prolonged malnutrition may stunt an individual's physical development, so a lack of the necessary experiences and opportunities may inhibit the young child's intellectual development. At the same time, not all deprived children are dull any more than all dull children are deprived. The presence in the urban sample of a number of DA children who appeared to be under-functioning relative to their estimated level of 'intelligence' has already been commented upon. It would seem, therefore, that although a highly intelligent child may succeed despite deprivation—and history provides numerous examples of this happening—the child of average or below average ability is highly susceptible to its ill effects. Educational attainment is particularly liable to suffer.

PROGRESS THROUGH THE INFANT SCHOOL

Detailed information on the children's reactions to the infant school programme and their adjustment and progress in the total school setting

29

was gathered in a series of six specially devised schedules, which were completed by the teachers for every child in the project at intervals throughout his or her time in the infant school. Four schedules were completed in the child's first year in school, one at the end of the first ten days in school and one at the end of each term. The other two schedules were completed at the end of the second and third years of infant schooling. The content of the schedules was adjusted each time so as to be appropriate to the levels which most of the children might be expected to have reached, but the items gave scope for variations in progress to be noted and were sometimes repeated over a number of schedules so that development over a period of time could be charted. Information was also obtained about the school organization, the methods of teaching and the problems most frequently encountered at the infant school stage.

Once again a pattern appears in the children's progress, although it is neither as clear nor as consistent as in their performance on the attainment test battery discussed in the previous section. It is difficult to say whether this blurring of the pattern is the result of genuine unevenness of development in the children or of different members of staff being involved in completing the schedules over the years or, most probably, a mixture of both of these. A further complication is the loss to the sample over the three years of a number of the children, a feature which was particularly noticeable in the DA group. Not only was the loss greater in that group but it also frequently occurred in the most deprived section of it, as it contained the families which, for a variety of reasons, were the most mobile. Therefore, while it is true to say that, in this study, there was no evidence of a progressive deterioration in performance such as has been found in American studies (e.g. Deutsch and Brown, 1964), it is arguable whether this is because of teachers having different standards in different school areas, or because of the loss of a number of children whose response to school might have been deteriorating, or because the effects of deprivation are not the same in this country as in America.

Language development

The typical finding for the urban sample, in many of the aspects covered, was of the children in the DA group trailing behind those in the CA group. Take, for example, the children's ability in language, a skill vitally important for successful adjustment to school. The DA group contained a higher proportion of children consistently rated as being restricted in the range of their spoken vocabulary than did the SWC or the MC groups. In the final schedule, where ability in written expression was rated, the same trend was in evidence. In articulation, the DA children at first received more of the lower ratings than the rest of the urban sample, although this aspect of their speech did appear to improve over the years. Some 'catching up' was also evident in their reception of language (i.e. ability to understand stories and to follow oral instructions).

Progress in reading

When progress in reading was examined, it was found that the MC children in the urban sample made a particularly good start. By the end of the first term, they were more advanced than either the SWC or the DA groups. In the course of the first year, however, the SWC children began to pull away from the DA children and the latter were consistently at a lower level of performance thereafter in all aspects of reading. A higher proportion of the DA children were still engaged in pre-reading activities when most of the rest of the urban sample had been promoted to coping with a reading scheme and, by the end of the third year, 38 per cent of the DA group had not reached Book IV (or its equivalent) in the scheme compared with 20 per cent of the rest of the urban sample. The rural children made a rather slow start in reading but caught up later with the urban sample. Indeed, few of the rural children were ever placed in the lowest rating categories for the various aspects of reading, although it must be remembered that the number of children involved was much smaller than in the urban sample.

The slower progress of the DA children in reading could have various explanations. It has already been said that their ability in language skills was less well developed than that of the more favoured urban children. It also seemed that the SWC children were more responsive to the school programme than the DA children, for they pulled away from the DA children in the course of the first year. These trends may reflect both a difference in parental attitudes to school in general or to language and reading in particular and a difference in the children's attitudes, inasmuch as there was evidence that the DA children were less interested in what school had to offer them and concentrated less well, especially in the first year. Children's progress in reading also reflects, of course, the attitudes of the teachers and the school policy. The teachers in the DA schools obviously felt that on entry some of their pupils had not reached a level of social, emotional or linguistic competence sufficient to enable them to deal with an introduction to reading proper. One DA class teacher expressed the feelings of many others when she said, 'These children have social and emotional needs which have to be met. They have no power of concentration, unlike children in other areas who may be ready for disciplined educational activities sooner'. In the DA schools, therefore, the children's introduction to the formal aspects of the basic skills was delayed and an informal programme with an emphasis on creative and expressive activities was implemented. The 'integrated day' approach was frequently adopted, while the CA schools were rather wary of total commitment to this form of organization and the RA schools, probably because of their wide age ranges in each class and more limited resources, did not favour it at all.

In the above comment no criticism is intended either of the schools or of the methods used. The informal, child-centred approach of the 'integrated day' form of organization has a great deal to commend it. But to ensure that every child benefits to the full from the experiences provided is a formidable task, especially with children who may have had very different pre-school experiences and who present uneven levels of development within and between themselves. Great care is required to be sure that children from disadvantaged areas do gain sufficient meaningful experiences in the activities particularly relevant to improving the skills, for example of language, in which they lag behind. The teachers in the DA schools were fully aware of the difficulties and, while the majority favoured the informal approach, they also fairly consistently pointed out the need for unobtrusive direction of children to specific activities and for a structuring of the progression within these activities to build up pre-reading skills.

What of the reading programme once children are able to proceed to it? In the first place, very little is known of the development of early reading skills in individual children. Another of the publications arising from the present research project attempts to chart this early development in two aspects of reading, word recognition skills and phonic knowledge (Davies and Williams, 1974). The results of the study indicate that children appear to go through three successive phases in their acquisition of these aspects of reading, the rate of acquisition of the skills varying considerably in each of the phases. It is still not possible to say what determines the different rates of growth. The implication of this for the devising of a suitable reading programme for DA children is obvious. If individual progress is uneven anyway, it is going to be particularly difficult to assess accurately the needs of children whose intellectual functioning may be affected by disadvantage. It could be noted in passing that the Swansea Test of Phonic Skills (Williams *et al.*, 1970) can offer some guidance to the teacher on individual levels of achievement in that particular aspect of reading.

In the second place, consideration must be given to the effect of the delayed start in reading which the DA children in this sample made, in comparison with the CA or the RA children. It may be that an increased provision of nursery school places will reduce the time which currently has to be given to raising the level of educational competence in children who have not had much chance in their early years. But until this can be shown to have happened, the problem for teachers in schools where there are children who are educationally 'at risk' must be how to use the time at their disposal most effectively. If the introduction of more formal work in reading has to be delayed, can the same approach to this formal work as used with non-deprived children be justifiably adopted? After all, the latter have not only been better prepared before school entry but they have also begun learning to read earlier.

In the present study, there seemed to be little difference in the approach made to the teaching of reading by the DA, CA and RA teachers. All schools used a combination of word recognition and phonic analysis, although the emphasis placed on one or the other differed from school to school. The 'Ladybird' series was the most favoured scheme, irrespective of the catchment area, and, although there were some adverse comments on the suitability of the content of the established reading schemes for DA children, remarks on the merits of the schemes outnumbered remarks on their faults in all groups. It certainly cannot be suggested that the DA children should be introduced earlier to reading proper if they cannot cope with it. But

33

the question could be raised as to how to proceed in order to accelerate the DA children's progress while ensuring that each element in that progress is firmly established.

Mathematical skills

When the children's performance in mathematical skills was considered, differences in the rates of progress in each group became evident but these differences were not very marked and not always in favour of the 'advantaged' urban children. The DA children had little difficulty in handling money, for example, unlike some of the more isolated RA children who seldom had this experience outside of school. It has already been noted, however, that at the end of the infant school period the rural children were superior in performance to the urban children as far as the test of the understanding of mathematical concepts was concerned. In all of the urban schools, modern approaches to the teaching of mathematics were adopted but the CA schools retained traditional approaches for part of the time, a practice which was even more common in the rural schools, perhaps because of the spread of ages in the smaller schools. It seems true to say, however, that the teaching of mathematics was not seen by any of the teachers in the present sample to involve the problems, either general or specific, met in the teaching of reading.

Play and creative activity

Among the most important experiences which the infant school programme offers to young children are opportunities for free play and creative activity. Was the response of the DA children to these opportunities similar to that of the other children? According to the information obtained from the various rating schedules, the initial reactions of the DA children appeared to be less purposeful and less imaginative than that of the rest of the children in the urban sample, presumably because the pre-school experiences of the latter (i.e. the CA group) were qualitatively superior. The DA teachers were alert to their pupils' needs and not only provided more opportunities for free play and creative experiences but also joined in the children's activities rather more frequently than the CA teachers, encouraging persistence and discussing possible end products. Initial differences in the reactions of the urban groups disappeared in the course of the first year. The RA children's reactions to free activities also reflected their pre-school experiences. Some of the RA children were shy and uncertain to begin with, unaccustomed to playing and communicating with other children. Again this initial response changed as the children settled in, but in some RA schools, because of staffing and space restrictions, there were fewer opportunities for the children to engage in self-chosen activities with the support of an interested adult. Over the course of the infant school period, however, the reaction shown by the children in the urban and rural samples came to reflect individual differences, in that some children were more creative and more responsive than others, rather than area type differences.

Adjustment to school

In the handling of play and creative materials, as in their language development, the DA children's early environment had not always been helpful to the school. What was its effect on their social and emotional adjustment? The answer to this question is complicated by the fact that, in one of the local authority areas studied, a number of nursery classes attached to existing infant schools had been established. Some of the DA children in the present study had attended and therefore were fairly familiar with their infant school and with school routine. (If the number of children with nursery attendance is considered, then the SWC group emerge as having the lowest per percentage (21%), but the overall DA percentage (33%) is far from representative of each of the 'deprived' areas studied.) Whether because of this complication or not, there seemed to be little difference in the children's early adjustment to the school situation. In the urban groups, and in the rural group, some children had problems but most settled in quickly. The DA children showed themselves to be quite as capable as the others of looking after themselves and their possessions; in fact they were rated more highly on these aspects than the SWC children.

Although the head teachers and teachers in the DA schools felt that children from 'disadvantaged' areas were often restless on entry to school, no more of the DA children were judged to be showing this

35

symptom than the CA children, as rated by their teachers. There did appear to be, however, a tendency for emotional and social difficulties to increase in the DA schools over the three years, whereas the opposite was true of the RA schools. Considerable attention was given by the research team to the sample children's adjustment both in school and at home, and a review of the findings can be found in the next chapter.

Prediction of progress in the junior school

One final point remains and that concerns the progress which the infant school teachers felt that their pupils would make in the junior school. The rural children were fortunate in this respect. Most of them remained in the same school and, although some of them presented problems of low attainment, change to a new class did not constitute any real break, as their needs were known and recognized. In the urban schools, it was felt that the DA group had a higher proportion of children who would be in difficulties in the junior school than the CA group, the main source of these difficulties being poor performance in the basic skills. Only occasionally were behavioural problems or immaturity mentioned. The results of the attainment testing at the end of the children's infant schooling would support the teachers' opinions. At the same time it must be remembered that children have a knack of conforming to what is expected of them. Some of the children in this study appeared to have more educational potential than they were using and this was especially true of a proportion of the DA group.

CONCLUSION

The purpose of the enquiries discussed in this chapter was to chart progress through the normal infant school programme and to see which aspects of that programme presented particular difficulties to some children. Although by no means all of the children living in unfavourable conditions did badly, the picture is not entirely encouraging, especially when it is remembered that the children in this sample were deliberately selected from an age band that had three full years of infant schooling.

Adequate verbal ability is probably the most important condition for success in our educational system as currently organized. It is particularly important in the infant school where reading and writing are beginning to be established. 'Adequate' does not necessarily mean that there is a fixed level of performance in verbal skills which children must reach before other skills can be introduced, but rather that they should be able to listen to language, to respond to it and to express what they want to say with clarity, confidence, accuracy and relevance. Obviously some will be better than others. What is worrying is when a disproportionately large number of children from favoured backgrounds are performing at a high level, while a disproportionately large number of children from unfavoured backgrounds are functioning at a low level.

Much of the discussion in this chapter has concerned progress in reading. Whether rightly or wrongly, most teachers, parents and children would consider this emphasis to be correct and would regard reading not just as the first R but as the all-important one at the infant school stage. The average performance of the DA children at the end of their infant schooling was less good than the teachers would have liked and meant that many of them were transferring to a new school at a point when reading was not securely established. Poor performance in reading appeared more than anything else to influence the teachers' judgements on the children's future progress (see also Evans, 1978). These are the reasons why the timing, and the nature, of the introduction of reading and its related skills to children from disadvantaged areas should be seriously discussed by teachers.

The performance and progress of the children through the typical infant school programme has been expressed in this chapter in terms of average rating and performance levels. As previously indicated, it would be wrong to conclude that every child from a disadvantaged area will do badly. It would also be wrong to conclude that disadvantage is the only reason for poor performance. Evidence from other work on the project, especially the work of the Identification Techniques Unit, highlights differences in performance related both to the child's home background and to his own abilities. However, where children can be identified as 'at risk' educationally because of disadvantageous home backgrounds, then there would seem to be justification for considering special programmes to be implemented as soon as possible after school entry. How successful such programmes would be, remains to be seen. What this chapter has shown is that, without such programmes, some children are not progressing as well as they might in the initial stages of their schooling.

4

Social Adjustment

It is always difficult to assess the significance of difficulties in social adjustment shown by infant school children at home or in the classroom, and to know when these are serious enough to warrant special attention. Many emotional and behavioural problems in young children, if handled with understanding, are of short duration. Some problems, in fact, are so common at this stage that they ought not to be regarded as necessarily indicating deviance or disturbance (Shepherd *et al.*, 1971). Nevertheless, not all the problems of young children resolve themselves easily, and even at the nursery stage the child with severe behaviour difficulties may be 'at risk' in regard to maladjustment later on (Westman *et al.*, 1967). Further, it is likely that the association found between poor adjustment and learning difficulties (Chazan, 1969) is often established in the infant school, since emotional problems can both lead to and result from learning failure. Children, for example, who are emotionally immature or disturbed in the reception class may make such a poor start in the mastery of basic scholastic skills that they find it difficult to recover, while those who, for reasons of intellectual or physical immaturity or a disadvantaged background, find school learning a burden even in the early stages may develop adjustment problems as a consequence. There is justification, therefore, for attaching increasing importance to the prevention of emotional and behavioural problems through early detection, careful diagnosis and appropriate action.

Our knowledge of the prevalence, nature and aetiology of behaviour problems in infant school children is limited, and little is known about the effects of material and cultural deprivation on the emotional and social development of children at this stage. It was, therefore, thought valuable to gather information, during the course of the project, on the prevalence of different kinds of behaviour problems shown by children in schools in 'deprived' areas; to enquire into the background and progress of the children in these schools who presented relatively severe problems of adjustment in their first year at school; to ascertain to what extent behaviour problems persisted throughout the three years of the infant school; and to discuss the views of both parents and

39

teachers on ways of dealing with behaviour problems in infant school children. This chapter will summarize the findings of the project relating to these questions.

PREVALENCE OF BEHAVIOUR PROBLEMS

Data on aspects of the emotional and social development of the whole sample of urban and rural children already described (see pp. 4–5) were obtained at intervals throughout the period of three years during which the children attended the infant school. In particular, information relating to the prevalence and nature of behaviour problems in the 'deprived' area (DA) sample, and, for purposes of comparison, the 'control' ('settled working-class' (SWC) and 'middle-class' (MC)) area children was provided on the third and sixth school schedules, towards the end of the first and final years of infant schooling respectively. In addition to an overall rating of the child's level of adjustment, based on that used by Schaefer as part of a Classroom Behaviour Inventory developed by him in the U.S.A. (unpublished to date), these two schedules included Stott's six adjustment pointers, which enable a general picture to be obtained, without undue trouble to the teacher, of the number of children in a given school or class whose response gives some cause for concern. The teachers of the rural children also provided the same kind of information as in the urban sample, and questions on the problems faced by the schools in dealing with emotional or behavioural difficulties shown by the pupils were included in the questionnaires completed by the heads and class teachers.

In the first year, according to the class teachers, as many as 24 per cent of the total sample of 725 children (355 'deprived', 309 'control' and 61 rural) aged between 5 years and 5 years 7 months showed *some* indication of behaviour deviating from the desirable norm, and approximately 13–14 per cent appeared to be presenting problems to an extent warranting attention, although only about 1 per cent were considered to need specialist help. Withdrawal and restlessness were the most common problems in the total sample, the boys presenting considerably more problems than the girls, particularly in respect of restlessness and aggressiveness. Similar results were obtained in the third year survey, which involved 602 children (279 'deprived', 265 'control' and 58 rural).

On both occasions, approximately 27 per cent of the 'deprived' area children scored at least one adverse Stott pointer, and 16 per cent were rated as 'somewhat' or 'very' disturbed. In the first year, there were no significant differences in the prevalence of behaviour problems between the DA and SWC children, but significantly more of the DA group presented problems than did the MC sample. The 'deprived' area children tended to display more aggressiveness and unsociability than the other children, and it was with problems arising from restlessness and aggressiveness that the DA schools were particularly concerned. However, at this stage, the differences in behaviour between the DA and other groups were not as great as might have been expected. There was a tendency, though not a very marked one, for the gap between the DA children and the 'control' area group (as a whole) to widen over the infant school period, in that the DA children were rated as displaying more extreme behaviour than the CA children to a greater extent in the second survey than the first. This seemed to reflect the tendency of the SWC group to be showing fewer gross behaviour problems at 7+ than at 5+, as, surprisingly, the gap between the DA and MC children was not as wide in the second survey as in the first. Although few significant differences emerged on either occasion between the urban and rural (RA) samples, there was a widening of the gap on most items between these groups also, the rural sample having few children with really severe problems (see Chazan and Jackson, 1971 and 1974 for further details of the results of the two surveys).

All the headteachers (14 DA, 12 CA and 10 RA) and class teachers (19 DA, 18 CA and 11 RA) attached great importance to the development of emotional and social maturity in their pupils, placing this above other educational aims such as the development of language skills or creativity, or scholastic progress. The estimates given by the headteachers of the prevalence of children in their schools presenting emotional, social or behavioural problems, either mild or serious, varied widely, ranging from 0 to 30 per cent in the case of mild problems, and from 0 to 18 per cent in the case of more serious difficulties. These estimates suggested, to a rather greater extent than the schedules completed by the class teachers, that the DA schools faced more difficulties relating to behaviour problems than the CA or RA schools.

The teachers in the different areas, asked to rank six types of problem behaviour in order of frequency of occurrence in their classes, all placed *restlessness* first, but whereas urban teachers ranked *aggressiveness* next, rural teachers felt that *shyness/withdrawal* was second in frequency, and 'deprived' area teachers placed *disruptive* and *unruly* behaviour higher than *nervousness* (e.g. timidity, tearfulness) which came at the bottom of their list. The DA and RA heads largely confirmed the ratings of the teachers in their schools, though the CA heads considered that nervousness rather than restlessness or aggressiveness was a particularly common problem.

Both the headteachers and the class teachers found most difficulty in coping with restlessness, aggressiveness and anti-social behaviour (e.g. lying, stealing, destructiveness). It would seem, therefore, that not only did the DA class teachers have a somewhat higher incidence of behaviour problems than the other groups, but the types of behaviour which occurred most frequently were the ones generally found most difficult to deal with.

ADJUSTMENT AND HOME BACKGROUND

Home background factors associated with poor adjustment in the infant school were examined mainly through an intensive study of 39 'poorly-adjusted' children (22 boys, 17 girls) selected in the first year from the total DA sample on the basis of their showing the most behaviour problems according to the Stott and Schaefer ratings. These children were compared with a control group of 42 'well-adjusted' children (24 boys, 18 girls), chosen from the same schools, who presented the fewest behaviour problems in the DA sample. The age, sex and social-class distribution of the two groups (henceforth referred to as the PA and WA groups) were similar. Completion of the Rutter Behaviour Scales by both teachers and parents confirmed that there was a highly significant difference in adjustment between the two groups at home as well as at school, even though the parents' and teachers' ratings showed considerable differences for many individuals.

Information on the children's early development and home background, as well as on the parents' use of services was obtained through three home visits. In most cases it was the mother who was interviewed, the level of co-operation and interest in the project being high. All the WA group had both parents at home; five PA children had only one parent.

Few differences between the groups emerged in respect of their early development. Slightly more of the PA group had been 'unwanted' or at least unplanned babies, and significantly more fathers in this group had been away from home for long periods. More of the PA children had speech difficulties, but the health problems of the two groups were similar. The PA children were more often unwilling to go to school.

Each home was rated on a 4-point scale on ten items, five relating mainly to material deprivation, five mainly of a cultural nature. Material factors rated were income; cleanliness of the home; housing conditions; play space; and the mother's care of the child. Cultural factors covered the mother's education; social class (based on father's occupation); the provision of play materials and books; the use of external stimuli; and the level of parental interest in the child's education. The comparison between the PA and WA groups showed that the PA children had a significantly more deprived background, both materially and culturally. The mothers of the poorly adjusted children had to manage on lower incomes, tended to be in poorer physical health, and coped less well with looking after the home. They had had more restricted educational opportunities themselves, and showed less interest in their children's school progress. The PA children were less well provided with books and toys as well as playspace within the home, and their parents read to them less. Although every family had a television set, the PA parents were less involved in their children's watching of television than the WA parents. The PA group, too, were less often taken on outings to such places as the park, cinema or zoo, and their parents had fewer interests or hobbies in which they could participate. There were thus fewer opportunities in the homes of the PA group for the children to keep themselves 'out of mischief' and to be stimulated intellectually.

As would be expected, the PA children were more demanding at home than the WA group, and the parents were more indulgent and more likely to give in to the children 'for the sake of peace'. No significant differences were recorded between the groups in the methods of rewards and punishment used by the parents. The majority of parents used smacking at least occasionally, and 'being sent to bed' was another commonly employed punishment or threat. Rather more than half of the parents from each group promised their children a reward for good behaviour or helpfulness, or gave the child an unexpected reward after being well-behaved. The PA parents, however, were less consistent in their handling of their children.

To sum up, the PA parents provided a much less secure, happy and settled home background for their children. While only six of the WA group came from homes which seemed not to be completely secure, well over half of the PA group came from homes rated as insecure in respect of both financial factors and the relationship between the parents. The PA mothers, too, tended to be less emotionally stable.

ADJUSTMENT AND SCHOOL PROGRESS

Already on entry to the infant school, the WA children were rated by their teachers as significantly ahead of the PA children in skills such as writing one's name or drawing simple objects. Later schedules showed a marked difference in favour of the WA group on many items relating to school achievement, such as pre-reading and reading skills, number, creative work and patterns of speech. This wide gap in attainments was consistently shown by the schedules throughout the three years of infant schooling, and was confirmed by the scores on the final test battery. The results of the standardized tests given in the third year revealed highly significant differences in mean scores between the groups in tests of reading, spelling, vocabulary and mathematics. The PA children were a year or more behind the WA group in all these aspects of school attainment and many of them had made very little progress at the time of testing.

Although the differences in the school progress of the two groups were very marked—and it is of interest to note how well the WA children, all living in deprived areas, were doing—it is difficult to know to what extent they can be attributed to differences in adjustment. There is a complex interaction between attainment, adjustment and general ability (or 'intelligence'), which factor, as measured by standardized tests, is an important one in school success, particularly in the primary school. Children of low intelligence may, *as a result* of their difficulties with school work, become restless, aggressive or withdrawn in class. It is relevant to ask, therefore, to what extent differences in intelligence in the two groups played a part. The PA group did, in fact, have somewhat lower scores than the WA children on the Raven's Coloured Progressive Matrices test and the NFER

44

Picture Test 'A', both of which may be regarded as non-verbal measures of intelligence. However, the mean scores of the PA group in these tests were within the average range, and statistical procedures adopted to control for intelligence indicated that the differences in the school performance of the WA and PA groups could not be attributed wholly to differences in general ability. Even on the basis of the scores actually obtained on the non-verbal intelligence tests, it seemed that the PA children were underfunctioning to a considerable extent; and it must be borne in mind that, in the case of poorly adjusted children, scores on intelligence tests tend not to give a true reflection of potential, since these children may not adapt easily to the test situation. Therefore, although the findings of this study concerning the school progress of the two groups need to be interpreted with caution, they suggest that children showing marked behaviour problems in their first year at school, even if they are of normal ability, are likely to be at risk of continued school failure.

PERSISTENCE OF BEHAVIOUR PROBLEMS

Behaviour problems in young children may well be transient, and poor adjustment is not necessarily a long-lasting handicap. It was of interest to ascertain to what extent initial ratings of children as presenting relatively severe problems were confirmed in their final year at infant school, and also whether those children whose problems did persist throughout the three years differed in any way from those whose problems appeared to have been resolved by the time they reached the end of their infant school.

In the total survey sample, when the persistence and development of poor adjustment was looked at in the individual cases of children who had remained in the sample throughout, it was found that, while a number of children improved in adjustment over the period, as many as 34 out of 80 children (42.5 per cent) who were rated as 'poorly adjusted' at 5+ on fairly strict criteria, still presented behaviour problems at 7+ years. In the intensive study, of the 36 children in the PA group who were rated again in their last year, 17 remained 'poorly adjusted' on the original criteria (3 + adverse Stott pointers *or* a Schaefer rating of 'very' or 'somewhat' disturbed), while 40 out of the 42 'well-adjusted' children were again rated in this category.

45

Thus, while the WA children remained a stable group, some of the PA children seemed to have resolved their problems by the third year. The 'persistent' members of the PA group had exhibited a greater number of problems or more severe difficulties at the earlier stage than those children who improved in adjustment. The main differences in the background of the 'persistent' and 'non-persistent' members of the PA group were on variables most directly related to school activities (e.g. the 'non-persistent' members were in a more favourable position regarding the use and provision of play materials and books, the extent to which the parents read to or played with the child, whether the parents encouraged curiosity, and the degree of contact between home and school). Those items relating to the more material factors in the home and, surprisingly, those reflecting its emotional atmosphere showed only small differences between the groups. These findings confirm that a lack of parental encouragement and a paucity of intellectual stimulation at home make it particularly difficult for a child to come to terms with the demands of school life.

USE OF SERVICES

A. *The school*

The general survey showed that, when asked to rate their pupils systematically, teachers identified a considerable number as presenting behaviour problems. Yet as many as 80 per cent of the class teachers stated either that they did not need any help in dealing with these problems, or that they were satisfied with the assistance already available. In most cases, they felt that problem behaviour could be dealt with internally, sometimes in consultation with colleagues or parents. Although some would welcome advice on coping with problem behaviour from outside agencies concerned with child welfare, referral to such agencies, for example the school psychological service, tended to be seen as a last resort. Only two children in the PA group were said to have received help from a child guidance clinic.

Some of the headteachers saw the need for more efficient liaison with existing services and more help from the social services, but on the whole the headteachers confirmed the view of the teachers that they would prefer to cope with behaviour problems by means of internal school resources, including aides and extra teachers, rather than by enlisting outside help. Although the rural schools in particular felt the lack of an educational psychologist on whom they could call if necessary, over a third of the heads were quite satisfied with the help available to them, which included the child guidance service, school medical officer, welfare officer, school nurse and the social services.

In spite of the reluctance on the part of the school to seek expert help for children with behaviour problems, it cannot be said that the teachers felt that all the problem behaviour which they observed in the child's early years was likely to be resolved easily. In the third year, 19 'poorly adjusted' children were assessed as 'almost certain to face difficulties in the junior school' because of behavioural and other difficulties.

B. *The parents*

Although many of the parents, particularly in the PA group, reported behaviour problems of various kinds at home, few were really worried about the behaviour or development of their children. Many parents, however, seemed to be very uncertain about what behaviour problems or habits were 'normal' at this age and frequently sought reassurance from the interviewer about this. About half of the total sample of parents, too, were rated as rather less than confident about the way they handled questions of discipline or problem behaviour. Many asked the interviewer about various methods concerned with bringing up children, and expressed doubt as to whether they as parents were doing 'the right thing'. Yet few parents had actually sought or received any help or advice on bringing up their children and, when specifically asked, only seven parents (3 PA and 4 WA) felt that any extra advice on handling children was necessary. Many of the families had little or no knowledge of the sources of help available in a crisis; for example, 26 PA and 21 WA parents were not aware of the service provided by child guidance clinics.

RELATED FINDINGS

The association between cultural and material deprivation in the home and poor adjustment in school found in Intensive Study B reported above was supported by a considerable overlap between the sample involved in that study (chosen on the basis of the extent of problem behaviour shown) and the sample selected in the other intensive study (A) described in Chapter 5 (chosen on the basis of degree of deprivation in the home). This link between deprivation and poor adjustment was also confirmed by the enquiry carried out by the Welsh Language Unit (Chapter 8).

Intensive Study A

This enquiry, while being particularly concerned with the effects of deprivation on language development, included an analysis of the differences in adjustment between the two samples selected, all living in 'deprived' areas but one group being from a relatively deprived home background (deprived group) and the other from a more advantaged background (control group). Assessments of the children's adjustment in school were made by means of the school schedules, which included the six Stott pointers, as well as the full Schaefer Classroom Inventory. On this basis, in both the second and third year of schooling, the deprived group showed poorer overall adjustment in school than the control group. It was of interest to attempt to ascertain when this gap between the two groups developed: was it already present at the time of school entry, or did it develop gradually afterwards? Evidence from the school schedules suggests that differences in adjustment in favour of the control group were to be seen at the time of school entry, but that they had become more marked by the end of the first term. However, there was little consistent evidence to suggest that thereafter the differences in adjustment between the two groups became more pronounced as the children progressed through the infant school. The data did not show any clear-cut differences in the patterns of behaviour shown by the two groups, but the deprived group tended to show less perseverance and poorer concentration in school tasks, and to be more withdrawn as well as more hostile to others.

Welsh-speaking children

The enquiry involving infant school children speaking Welsh as their first language, carried out by the Welsh Language Unit, looked at differences in school adjustment in the samples of 'deprived' (Dep) and relatively more advantaged (Con) children. In the first year, the school schedules showed that a significantly greater number of Dep children were exceptionally quiet or withdrawn, and more of them displayed behaviour which was not expected of a normal alert child; an overall assessment showed the Dep group to be less well adjusted than the Con group to a highly significant extent. At 7 +, evidence from Rutter's Child Scale B and the school schedules showed continued differences in adjustment, in some respects, between the two groups, the Dep group being in particular less co-operative with other children, more solitary, and less able to concentrate on activities of a more structured kind. However, the gap in adjustment between the two groups had lessened to some extent during the infant school period.

SUGGESTIONS FOR ACTION

The enquiries undertaken by the project were not designed to discover or evaluate any procedures to alleviate problems of behaviour at the infant school stage. However, the information obtained from these investigations, which emphasize that within the 'working-class' a wide variety of attitudes and practices is to be found, may serve as a basis for making suggestions about the kinds of action which might be taken to help infant school children with problems of adjustment. Apart from measures designed to deal with behaviour difficulties when they occur in the classroom, the association between poor adjustment and deprivation found in the project's enquiries suggests that helping children from deprived backgrounds to make an easy transition from home to the school setting will help to reduce the incidence of behaviour difficulties. The discussion here will consider how both parents and school may be given help and support.

Parents

Home background factors have been shown to be related to the child's initial adjustment to school. It is relevant to ask, therefore, how parents can be helped to provide an environment which will prepare the child socially and emotionally for life at school. Undoubtedly, there are many

49

parents who already provide their children with an appropriate environment, and in addition there are a large number who, although they may not provide what might be regarded as the 'ideal' setting for the child's fullest development, are quite unaware of any need for help. The number who actively seek help or feel an unmet need for help is surprisingly small.

Two main approaches seem desirable here. One is to provide, more systematically than at present, 'education for parenthood', beginning on a formal basis in the secondary school and continuing to be available in the adult years. The other is to make access to the various helping agencies easier and more rewarding.

Education for parenthood starts early in the child's life, when he observes his own parents' actions, and the way in which the child (and later the adolescent) is handled by his parents is probably the most important factor in his preparation for being a parent himself. However, the secondary school can contribute to this preparation by encouraging discussions, for example, about adolescence and issues worrying adolescents. Older secondary school pupils can benefit from a practical study of child development, for example by visiting nurseries, play groups and nursery schools. Courses on child-rearing organized in colleges of further education or university extramural departments are valuable, as are classes and discussions arranged at ante-natal and post-natal clinics. In this work psychologists and psychiatrists can make a contribution by taking the initiative in organizing experimental courses, by giving talks and leading discussions, by acting as consultants and by helping to train group leaders.

Although considerable progress has been made in providing help and guidance for parents in bringing up their children, much more remains to be done, not least in making existing services more effective. Apart from the provisions for financial assistance and free school meals, the functions of the various helping services are not widely or accurately known by parents in deprived areas. Services such as child guidance or speech therapy are not known to many parents, not even to some of those who have experienced a definite need for help. It is important, therefore, that the local authority should, by all possible means, ensure that the facilities available to families in need are widely known, and it is also desirable that, when seeking help from the social, medical or psychological services, parents should not be made to feel embarrassment or undue frustration. In addition to the diagnostic and treatment services provided by child guidance clinics for the more serious problems of adjustment referred to them, there is a need for a comprehensive counselling service for parents, with the emphasis on preventing developmental difficulties and on enabling parents to understand how they can support their children's efforts in school. It would be appropriate that a counselling service of this kind should have very close links with nursery and infant schools. This would help to bridge the gap between home and school which contributes to the poor adjustment of some children in deprived areas. Children may present problems in school without the parents being aware of any difficulties, or at home without the teachers knowing, and regular discussions between parents and teachers—sometimes together with psychologist or psychiatrist—will bring to both a better understanding of a child's development.

The School

The enquiries conducted by the project have shown that, with systematic screening procedures, even of a simple kind, teachers can identify infant school children at risk of both maladjustment and school failure. While it is important that the significance of behaviour problems at this stage should not be 'labelled' in any rigid way, the fact that a number of children not only remain poorly adjusted throughout the three years of infant school, but are also at risk of continued learning difficulties, suggests that more attention should be given to their problems. To this end, teachers need more guidance in recognizing signs of poor adjustment, in dealing with behaviour problems in the classroom, and in knowing when to request outside help.

It has been shown that teachers frequently regard calling on external agencies as a 'last resort'. This is probably in part because they wish to deal with the problems of their pupils themselves, and do not want to acknowledge an inability to cope with these, and also because the outside agencies are often viewed as somewhat remote from the school. For example, the Social Services Department, being administered separately from the local education authority, may not have close links with the schools; the school psychological service may be able to devote only a very limited amount of time to infant schools. If they are to be effective, the helping agencies must be seen by the schools to be real partners. They must also be prepared to work within the school as well as outside it. With the development of the school psychological service in Britain, there has indeed been a tendency for the educational psychologist to spend more time in the school than in the office or clinic; but, as previously stated, because of pressures from junior and secondary schools, few educational psychologists are able to devote much time to infant schools. At present, with the reorganization of the health services in Britain, there are indications that child guidance clinics will strengthen their links with other community services. Useful models of comprehensive and community-centred approaches to prevention and treatment of developmental difficulties have been provided by projects in the U.S.A., for example in South Carolina (Newton and Brown, 1967) and Woodlawn, Chicago (Schiff and Kellam, 1967).

Within the classroom, infant school teachers are usually well aware of the desirability of giving more individual attention to children with problems, but large classes make this difficult. Apart from reduction in the size of classes, particularly necessary in schools in deprived areas, additional para-professional staff such as teachers' aides considerably help here.

Some children will need rather more attention than can be given by the class teacher, even with an assistant to help her. Although some teachers may not welcome even specialist aid within the classroom, the availability of peripatetic teachers specifically trained in dealing with problem children may help to reduce pressures when a class contains a number of difficult children. Several local education authorities in Britain have begun experiments in providing teachers of this kind, as well as in establishing special classes or nursery-type units for children who do not fit into infant school life. The Inner London Education Authority, for example, has set up 'nurture groups' designed for very immature children, particularly in inner city schools. These groups are run on a semi-domestic basis, the principles of care being those of the mother with her young child, though with the aim of orientating the children towards a return to normal school life (Boxall, 1973). Experiments of this kind, which aim at providing help for children with difficulties, yet are firmly based in the ordinary school, merit wide replication.

Problems of poor adjustment at the infant school stage should not be exaggerated. Children are very adaptable and the majority, coming from all kinds of home background, enjoy and benefit from their infant schooling, even if the process of adjustment takes a little time. Nevertheless, a not negligible minority of children, especially those from disadvantaged homes, fail to adjust to the infant school. We need to know much more about how to help this group. It would be valuable to observe the effects of early screening procedures used in the infant school, followed by guidance to both teachers and parents of children identified as 'at risk'. We need to increase our knowledge, too, about the effects of different approaches on children with different kinds of behaviour problems. However, it is suggested here that a great deal can be done, through the collaboration of home, school and the helping agencies, to prevent serious problems of emotional and social adjustment from developing at the infant school stage, or at least to minimize their effects.

5
Language Skills

As previously described, the Emotional Development and Response to Schooling Units of the project carried out a longitudinal study of the school progress and adjustment of a large sample of children in infant schools serving 'deprived areas' (DA schools). Many aspects of the development of these children were studied, but in the present chapter, only the findings regarding language development will be presented (see Chapter 3 for a discussion of the overall findings).

In addition to the above general study, one of the two intensive studies (Intensive Study A) carried out on sub-samples of children drawn from the main sample, examined the effects of cultural and material deprivation in the home background upon the children's development, and the findings concerning oral language skills will be reported in the second part of this chapter. Finally, the main conclusions of the two studies concerning language development will be presented and the educational implications of these discussed.

The growth of oral language skills in children was a major focus of interest in the two studies, particularly the intensive study. The importance of language in facilitating concept formation and thinking has been well attested by Vygotsky (1962) and Bruner (1964), whilst Luria (1961) has stressed its importance in helping the child to gain control of his overt behaviour. During the infant school years children develop basic concepts such as those of number and class which form the foundation for mathematical and logical thinking, and language plays an important part in this development. The growth of efficient reading skills depends upon a basis of an adequate vocabulary and command of the grammatical structures that children are likely to encounter. Moreover, oral language is of exceptional importance during the infant school stage, not only because it enables the child to develop other basic educational skills but also because it is the main teaching medium, whereas in later years the written word assumes relatively greater importance.

The ratings which the teachers were asked to make in respect of the project children tapped both the expressive and receptive (or comprehension) aspects of oral language skills. The expressive skills rated were speech articulation, range of spoken vocabulary and fluency of oral language. The receptive skills were the ability to follow oral instructions and stories. The ratings were based on three or four-point scales as in the following example:

please rate the quality of the child's speech articulation	very clear, precise and well-articulated	1
	quite clear on the whole, but may show some faulty enunciation	2
	difficult to understand because of marked immaturity; poor enunciation; over-rapid speech	3

These and other ratings were incorporated into a series of questionnaires or school schedules, which were completed by the class teachers at the end of the children's first and second terms, and subsequently towards the end of their first, second and third school years.

Expressive language skills

On the expressive language ratings the 'control area' (CA) sample showed clear and consistent superiority over the 'deprived area' (DA) sample on each occasion. When the 'settled working-class' (SWC) area children who formed part of the CA sample, were compared separately with the DA children, the differences followed the same pattern as in the main comparison (CA *vs* DA) but were less pronounced. The finding that the CA children were rated as using a more extensive spoken vocabulary than the DA children was supported by the result of a standardized vocabulary test administered in the children's final infant school term as part of the attainment survey. On this test the CA children had a significantly higher mean score than the DA

55

children, this difference being maintained when the 'middle-class' (MC) area children were removed from the CA sample and the SWC area children compared directly with the DA children. In this test the children were asked to give oral definitions of a series of words graded in difficulty, such as 'bicycle', 'nuisance' and 'gamble'.

Whilst this chapter is concerned with oral language skills, it is interesting to note that the relative superiority of the CA children in their expressive language appeared to extend to the written word also. During the third term of the children's final infant school year the class teachers were asked to rate the quality of the children's sentence construction in their written language. It was found that the CA children received significantly better ratings than the DA children, and this difference was maintained when the MC area children were removed from the CA sample and the results re-analysed.

In terms of standardized scores on the vocabulary test referred to earlier, the CA children performed at a level corresponding to their chronological age (although the MC area children's mean vocabulary age was one year above that of the SWC area children), whilst the mean vocabulary age of the DA children was six months below their mean chronological age. This finding should be regarded with caution, though, because the test was standardized on American children.

Receptive language skills

In the case of the receptive language skills of understanding stories and following oral instructions, the pattern of results obtained was rather different from that described above. Although, on both items, the CA children had consistently higher ratings than the DA children over the series of school schedules, the difference between the two groups fell below statistical significance in the final schedule (end of third year) in the case of ability to follow oral instructions, and at the end of the second and third years respectively in the case of understanding orally presented stories. The trend of results was similar when the SWC area children in the CA group was compared directly with the DA children, except that the differences between the ratings received by these two groups on following oral instructions did not reach statistical significance at any stage during the three years. It seems, therefore, that in these skills the DA children tended to make greater progress relative to the CA children during the final year, possibly because their experience in school of stories and carrying out oral instructions may have made up for any earlier deficiencies in such experience at home. This interpretation must be made with caution, however, since the size of the research sample dropped over the period covered by the school schedules, and there was some evidence of selective losses from the DA sample in particular, i.e. the children who transferred from the project schools to other infant schools tended to be rather poorer in basic attainment than the DA children in general.

The teachers' views

The above findings were supported by the results of interviews with the headteachers and the class teachers responsible for the project children during their first school year, carried out as part of the general study. The teachers were asked, among other things, whether they experienced any problems in teaching their children oral language skills. Whilst the majority of the CA schools reported no real difficulties, the DA school teachers considered that they faced serious language problems regarding their children, including poor speech articulation and listening skills, limited vocabulary and self-expression, and an impoverished background' of stories and rhymes. The following is a sample of comments made by DA class teachers concerning the language of their children at school entry. The children:

> 'lack adequate language experience. They haven't been anywhere or done anything'
> 'are not able to speak in properly constructed sentences at first. For instance, at news time a child says "tank". I tell him to say, "I've got a tank at home", but he simply repeats, "tank"'
> 'won't talk to or even answer the teacher on entry and they usually take a few weeks to open up. Their speech is not clear and sometimes it is incomprehensible, but speech therapy is regularly available'.

Comparison with previous work

On the whole the findings of the general study are in line with the results of research into social class differences in language skills.

57

McCarthy (1954), summarizing the literature on this question, considered that there was a strong relationship between social class status and the child's language development, in favour of 'middle-class' children. She concluded that these widespread and important differences might to some extent be due to the more restricted environment of 'working-class' children and the poorer quality of parental language models available to them. More recent surveys (e.g. Deutsch 1965; Davie *et al.*, 1972) have confirmed this pattern of social class differences in language development.

The particular interest of the findings of the general study, however, lies in the fact that they show that differences in language performance are apparent not only *between* 'middle-class' and 'working-class' children, but also, on a reduced scale, *within* a large group of 'working-class' children, i.e. the SWC area children were rated as superior in their language skills to the DA children. This finding is in line with the results of some other recent research. The National Child Development Study (Pringle *et al.*, 1966; Davie *et al.*, 1972), for example, showed that there were differences in school attainment among subgroups of 'working-class' children (especially between children coming from skilled 'working-class' families and those whose fathers were in unskilled occupations) as well as between 'middle' and 'working-class' children.

INTENSIVE STUDY A

Given that working-class children show a wide range of variation in their level of language and other educational skills, it is important to ask whether a similar range of achievement can be found among children attending schools in 'deprived' catchment areas. In order to answer this question an intensive study of a sub-sample of children drawn from the general study sample was carried out. A further reason for carrying out a more intensive study stems from the fact that social class as such is a rather crude index of the level of cultural provision in a child's home. As Jensen (1967) points out, the assessment of social class status depends largely upon 'non-psychological' variables such as the father's occupation or income, and these may not relate very closely to the educational quality of the home environment. What we need in studying home background influences upon children's development are more sensitive measures of the level and quality of the cultural provision provided by the parents, and of the attitudes of parents towards their children's education. Some major British studies (e.g. Fraser, 1959; Douglas, 1964 and the Plowden Report, 1967) have shown the importance of positive parental attitudes for the adequate development of children's abilities. The survey of parental attitudes carried out for the Plowden Report showed that such attitudes were to a large extent independent of parental social class status (Plowden Report, Volume II, Appendix 4). It was not possible in the context of the general study to obtain such measures of parental attitude, or of the level of cultural provision in the children's homes, because of the limited resources of the project, but this was feasible with the intensive study sub-sample.

Design of study

For the reasons stated above, it was decided to draw a sub-sample of children from 'deprived area' schools in the main sample, and to study their home backgrounds and their development in much greater depth than was possible in the general study. The main hypotheses of this study were as follows:

(i) that cultural and material deprivation in the home would have adverse effects upon infant school children's development in the school setting, and that these effects, whilst very wide-ranging, would be particularly evident in the field of language, and in cognitive and educational skills;

(ii) that there would be evidence of an increasing gap in performance between culturally deprived children and more advantaged children as they progressed through their infant schools, due to the cumulative nature of deprivation effects.

The study sample comprised fifty-two pairs of infant school children matched for age, sex and school, and approximately matched on a measure of non-verbal intelligence, but differing in that one member of each pair came from a relatively deprived home background, in the cultural and material sense, and the other from a more advantaged background. The assessment of each child's home was made by the project's social worker, using a specially devised parental interview questionnaire. Information on the home background was collected under the broad headings of cultural and material factors, and within these, ratings were made on a series of features (already described in Chapter 4, see page 43). Thus, the sample consisted of a Deprived Group and a Control Group of children, and was drawn from schools in three urban areas nominated by the LEAs concerned as serving 'deprived' catchment areas. Therefore the great majority of the children came from 'working-class' backgrounds. The sample was drawn up towards the end of the children's first school year and was studied over the following two years of their infant school careers.

The study concentrated on language skills, but within a fairly comprehensive scheme of assessment which included concept formation, visual perception, motor co-ordination, motivation and aspects of personality. Assessments were made mainly by individually administered tests, some of which were devised for this study. The aspects of language tested were classified as structural or functional. Structural aspects comprised speech (auditory discrimination, articulation and sound blending), vocabulary, grammar and syntax, and sentence formation. Functional aspects comprised classification, description, oral comprehension and narration. In addition to the test data, information on the children's oral language skills was obtained by means of the teachers' ratings which were included in the school schedules used in the general study.

Results

It was found that the Control Group achieved significantly higher scores on the majority of the language tests, covering a wide range of language abilities, from simpler skills such as speech articulation and grammatical usage to more complex skills such as grasp of sentence structure and the use of language for describing and classifying. Contrary to this general trend, however, the two groups were not well differentiated on measures related to a story re-telling task requiring the use of sequential language, although the Control Group obtained higher mean scores on most of these. It had been expected that the performance of the Control and Deprived groups in this task would reflect, fairly clearly, Bernstein's (1971 a, b) distinction between elaborated and restricted language codes, but this was not the case.

On the other hand, the linguistic quality of the children's stories varied very considerably as the following examples show (the children were asked to re-tell a story based upon Aesop's fable of the dog and a bone which they had just listened to, and their stories were tape-recorded and subsequently transcribed without punctuation):

(i) A dog—man—meat—bone—a man—two dogs—dog—a bone —trees—a dog—bone—grass—dog—bone—dog and bone— he dropped his bone and a dog.

(ii) The dog went to the butcher's he ran out the house and he and they couldn't find him so he was in the butchers get find he went to get a bone and then the butcher creeped and got behind the bar and then he gave him the bone and then he then he run out the shop and then he the man couldn't catch him so the children run after him and he got near this he said shall I eat my bone or cos I'm so thirsty so he went to this big water puddle (repeated) and he looked down and the and there was another dog looking up to him he had a bone a big bone and he thought shall I bark and he'll drop his and I'll get it so the dog barked and then he dropped it right in the water and the dog never got it.

(iii) Once—this story is about a dog named Bouncer he was a naughty dog he always got up into mischief one day he was walking along the street and saw a butcher's shop he went in and he saw a customer and he said and he thought good and he nipped behind the counter where all the bones were thrown and saw a nice juicy bone waiting for him and he picked it up in his mouth and ran out of the butcher's house and the butcher ran after him and by the time he had got to the door he was round the corner the people saw him and said look at that dog with a nice with a big bone some children ran after him but the dog could run faster than the children he went through the forest to some woods and he wondered if he should eat his bone now but he was thirsty and tired and he saw a stream with a bridge across them—and he went and looked down and saw a another bone another dog with a bone and he said and he thought that dog's got a bigger bone than me I'll fight for it so he barked and he's the one who lost the bone and he was a very sad dog and he went home and lied in his

61

front garden wondering if I'd just been content and I would have be eating that juicy bone right now.

The results of the teachers' ratings of the children's oral language skills supported the general pattern of the test findings for they showed the Control Group to be consistently and significantly superior to the Deprived Group in all aspects rated. These results are also in line with the general study finding reported earlier that, on the same ratings of language skills, the CA children were judged to be markedly better than the DA children.

On the repeat administration of a language test designed to assess the child's grasp of basic sentence forms (Watts' English Language Scale), after a one year interval, the Control and Deprived Groups were not significantly differentiated, whereas they had been on the first occasion of testing (the Control Group being superior in mean score). Similarly, the difference between the two groups fell below significance on a vocabulary test given during the children's final infant school term, whereas, on similar vocabulary tests administered during the previous two years, the Control Group obtained markedly higher scores than the Deprived Group. Taken together, these two findings support the contention that, at least in these aspects of language development, the gap in level of achievement between the two groups diminished somewhat over time, although this interpretation was complicated by the nature of the loss of children from the sample during the period of the study. Moreover, it was not supported by a similar 'closing of the gap' in the teachers' ratings of the children's language skills made over the three years of the children's infant schooling, except, possibly, in the case of oral language skills. Certainly, however, there was no indication of an increasing disparity in language proficiency between the two groups over time, as had been predicted on the basis of some previous research, e.g. the survey by Deutsch (1965) referred to earlier in this chapter.

In terms of language attainment ages, obtained by reference to standardized test norms, where these were available, the Control Group performed at an average level for their age on two administrations of a 'receptive' measure of vocabulary (Brimer and Dunn, 1962), but below average on two 'expressive' vocabulary measures (requiring word definitions), though it must be remembered that the latter were normed on American children. On the other hand, the Deprived Group children performed well below average on all of the vocabulary measures. This relatively poor performance of the Deprived Group children may reflect the failure of the home backgrounds of these children to provide a sufficient variety and number of experiences necessary to stimulate the development of a rich vocabulary, and also, perhaps, the lack of parental encouragement to label and verbalize these experiences. Some of the vocabulary test responses of the Deprived Group children showed a marked verbal poverty in comparison with those of the Control Group children, as illustrated in the following examples of children's definitions of the test word 'umbrella':

Control Group	*Deprived Group*
1. 'It stops the rain—you put it over your nead—it's got a handle to hold it up.'	'hold' (Q) 'up'
2. 'Something to keep the rain off you and if it's windy it could blow inside out.'	'rain' (Q) 'snow'

'Q' indicates that a supplementary question was asked by the examiner.

On two sub-tests of the Illinois Test of Psycholinguistic Abilities, a test involving description of simple objects and a sound blending test, the Control Group children obtained language attainment ages well above the (American) norms but on a test of grammatical usage from the same battery they fell a little below the norm. The Deprived Group children performed at a below-average level for their age on all three tests.

Thus, according to the above measures at least, the Deprived Group children were not only inferior in language proficiency to the Control Group children but were also somewhat retarded in their language development compared with representative samples of children, although in some cases these were composed of American children.

The study also showed that the Deprived Group children performed poorly in comparison with their controls on tests requiring the use of language for classifying objects or situations. In one of these tests, for example, the child was presented with a series of pictures and was asked to give one word that best described each picture. The pictures portrayed actions, such as sewing, categories or collections such as furniture, and composite scenes such as a farmyard. The child's responses were scored according to their degree of abstraction and relevance to the picture. It was found that the Control Group children performed better on this test than the Deprived Group children, particularly in those sections requiring the naming of scenes and collections. The results of this and other classifying tasks used in this study are in accordance with previous research findings, and support the view of some writers that disadvantaged children are especially limited, in comparison with their more advantaged peers, in the more abstract uses of language (e.g. Tough, 1973) and the formation of 'higher order' concepts (Deutsch, 1965). It seems likely that the homes of disadvantaged children will be relatively deficient not only in the provision of the experiences upon which a child's conceptual learning must be based, but also in the corrective feedback from adults necessary for the sharpening and refining of concepts.

As mentioned earlier, the intensive study examined other aspects of children's development besides oral language skills. These included reading, spelling and mathematics, concept formation (number), visual perception, motor co-ordination, concentration, and social and emotional adjustment in school. It was found that, although the results of the tests and teachers' ratings were mostly in the expected direction, i.e. favouring the Control Group children, in some cases the mean difference between the two groups was rather small and fell well below statistical significance. In the light of these results it seems reasonable to state that, although the Deprived Group were markedly poorer than their Control Group partners on a wide range of school-related measures, the most consistent and pronounced differences emerged in the area of oral language skills.

Comparison with previous work

With the exception of the findings on the story retelling task, the results of the intensive study are in line with previous research findings on the relation between social class and language development outlined earlier in this chapter, and with the findings of the general study already described. Whilst the general study showed that the language skills of children attending 'deprived area' schools were markedly poorer than those of children in the CA schools, the intensive study showed that, even *within* the 'deprived area' school sample, children from relatively more advantaged homes were more advanced in language and other school-related skills than children from relatively deprived homes. The latter finding is supported by the results of recent research studies, both in this country and the U.S.A., which have also focussed upon samples of children specifically defined as culturally or socially disadvantaged. For example, Phillips, Wilson and Herbert (1972) studied a sample of six- to seven-year-old boys from highly socially-handicapped families (the Focus Group) and control groups of boys from families showing moderate or low degrees of social handicap respectively, according to a specially devised index which included ratings of social class, school attendance, size of family, condition of children's clothing and frequency of contact between teacher and parents. The Focus Group all came from families known to the city's Children's Department which were characterized by a fairly high degree of unemployment and low income.

The Focus and Control samples were drawn from predominately 'working-class' families, and the children lived in the 'twilight' inner-ring areas of Birmingham and attended the same schools. The Focus Group was compared with the controls on several psychological and educational tests, and significant differences in favour of the latter children were found. Moreover, on some of the psychological measures, including vocabulary development, a consistent and orderly relation-ship between degree of social handicap and level of development was found (low handicap being associated with high test score and vice versa). Furthermore, whilst the control boys performed at an average level for their age on the vocabulary tests, the performance of the Focus boys was well below average.

Another British study was that carried out by Tough (1971, 1973, 1977a) into linguistic differences between two small groups of three-year-old children of above average intelligence, one group coming from a favoured home background with respect to the fostering of language skills, and the other from a less favoured background. A sample of the children's language was obtained by recording each child's speech in a standardized play situation and this speech sample was analysed for complexity of speech structure and other features. The 'favoured' group used more complex language structures than the 'less favoured' group, and also showed a greater tendency to use language for such purposes as enlisting the co-operation of others, for conveying infor-mation not apparent in the immediate concrete situations, and as a vehicle for imaginative play.

The main conclusion which can be drawn from both the studies described above is that cultural and material deprivation in the child's home background has adverse effects upon his development in the school setting, particularly in the area of language and related skills. This conclusion is supported by the fact that the headteachers and class teachers in the DA schools, unlike their colleagues in the CA schools, considered that they faced serious difficulties in teaching their children relevant language skills because of the limited language powers and impoverished linguistic background of these children.

The second conclusion is that, contrary to expectation, the performance gap between children from relatively deprived home backgrounds and those from more advantaged backgrounds did not increase during the three-year period of infant schooling, and actually appeared to diminish in respect of some language skills. This finding could be regarded as reflecting the 'compensatory' effect of schooling upon the abilities of children from culturally deprived backgrounds, but it should be borne in mind that the period of the study was relatively short and that, in the long term, the performance gap might increase. Moreover, even at the end of their infant school careers, a substantial proportion of these children were seriously backward in vocabulary, reading and spelling skills.

The implications of the main findings of the two studies are twofold. The first concerns the concept of a 'deprived area'. The general study showed that wide differences in language and related skills appear to exist among 'working-class' families, these differences probably reflecting, at least in part, home background factors such as parental attitude to education and the general quality of cultural provision in the home. The intensive study showed that similar differences could be found within the relatively narrow confines of a 'deprived' school catchment area, even when the children were matched for important characteristics such as age, sex, and intelligence. The general study findings lend support to the administrative usefulness of the Plowden Report's concept of a 'deprived area' in that the schools in the sample which served such areas showed a higher incidence of educational backwardness and other problems, compared with schools serving more favoured areas. However, the findings of the intensive study point up the dangers inherent in labelling whole areas as 'deprived', and indicate the importance of identifying the particular *families* within such areas (and even in more favoured areas) where there is inadequate preparation and support for a child's schooling and, in consequence, the child could be described as educationally 'at risk'. The Identification Techniques Unit of the project has developed techniques for the early identification of such children (see Chapter 2).

The second implication stems from the finding that, compared with their more advantaged peers, children from deprived home backgrounds showed a lower level of performance in a wide range of language skills, but particularly in the use of language as a means of classifying and organizing their experience. This implies that these children need special help in developing more competence in these language skills, which are crucial to general educational progress. The nature of such help will be discussed in the following chapter, but it is necessary to consider, first, the validity of the finding of the intensive study in the light of recent controversies regarding the nature of cultural disadvantage.

The view that children from lower 'working-class' or certain cultural minority group backgrounds are deficient in important aspects of linguistic and cognitive skills has been strongly challenged by linguists and socio-linguists such as Bernstein (1969) and Labov (1970), who argue that the language deficits of such disadvantaged children are more apparent than real and that, potentially at least, such children *can* use more 'elaborated' language forms and handle logical or abstract relations.* However, they are not predisposed to do so in the school setting or the formal test situation because such contexts are rather alien to them and, therefore, inhibiting. In addition to low motivation, further factors likely to depress the school or test performance of these children are differences in language patterns (dialects) between teachers or testers and the children, and the fact that the content of what is being taught or assessed may be 'middle-class' and unfamiliar. Some might argue, in addition, that teachers in schools serving deprived areas may have lower expectations of the children they teach than are appropriate, and that these may act in a self-fulfilling fashion to depress the educational achievement of disadvantaged children.

It may well be that factors of the kind just discussed operate to inflate

* For a more recent discussion of this question, see Davis, A. (ed., 1977). *Language and Learning in Early Childhood.* London: Heinemann.

the differences in language performance between culturally disadvantaged and other children revealed in the research studies described in this chapter. However, these factors are unlikely to explain away such differences entirely, for, although a child may *potentially* be able to develop the use of language at abstract levels, he needs the guidance and encouragement of adults in order to realize this capacity and such guidance will tend to be lacking in disadvantaged homes. As Tough (1973, p. 70) puts it, 'It seems likely that there are some uses of language that the child rarely meets, and which his interaction with other people rarely provokes. In other words, the child makes low scores because he is disposed to use language for purposes which can be adequately served without complex or elaborating structures.' Moreover, the use of language as a system for abstracting and organizing experience requires a basis of relevant concrete experience upon which fundamental concepts, such as those of class, number and causality, can be built. Again, the deprived home background is one in which such experiences are lacking or insufficient.

The challenge facing formal education is to develop in disadvantaged children both the ability and the motivation to use elaborated language to facilitate learning and thinking. But any educational programme with such aims should be applied in the light of awareness by teachers of the patterns of language use which characterize the sub-cultures of deprived children. It should be realized that, as linguists have stressed, the language forms used by the children are fully adequate for normal communication purposes *within* those sub-cultures, and should not be denigrated by the school. The following chapter discusses various approaches to the teaching of language skills to disadvantaged young children, with particular reference to the approach to this problem adopted by the Programme Development Unit of the present project. The work of that Unit was guided in part by the findings of the intensive study of the Emotional Development and Response to Schooling Units summarized in this chapter.

6

Fostering Language Development

Given that children from disadvantaged home backgrounds are relatively slow to develop the language skills necessary for them to perform efficiently in school, the question arises as to how they can be helped to attain such skills more quickly. In the course of the general study reported in the first part of Chapter 5, headteachers and classteachers were asked in what ways they would like to extend the opportunities available to their children for developing oral language skills. All of the Control Area (CA) school teachers interviewed considered that their children were getting sufficient practice for their needs in speaking and listening, but about half of the Deprived Area (DA) school teachers felt their children needed more practice. However, both CA and DA teachers made suggestions for the extension of oral language work in schools, and these were mostly aimed at yielding more time for the class teacher to converse and interact with children, individually or in groups. The suggestions included a more generous teacher–pupil ratio, the introduction of teacher-aides into the classroom, and the more extensive use of audio-visual aids such as the tape recorder.

It seems unlikely, however, that the greater teacher–pupil contact facilitated by such measures will achieve a significant advance in the development of disadvantaged children's oral language unless teachers are quite clear about their aims in such teaching, and plan appropriate language experiences for their children more or less systematically. It is interesting, in this connection, that despite the general superiority of the CA children over the DA children in oral language skills, the teaching approach prevailing in the two groups of schools was basically the same, i.e. all of the schools adopted an informal 'general enrichment' approach to language development, based upon discussion and conversation arising from normal classroom activities and incidental correction of faulty language responses. In other words, no school appeared to follow a systematic language programme with clearly specified objectives and specially planned language activities.

Both in Britain and the United States controversy surrounds the question of whether the teaching of language skills in young children should take place in a fairly structured or relatively unstructured setting (see, for example, Quigley, 1971). Some educationists, probably including teachers in the schools referred to above, feel that such skills should be developed informally and incidentally, in the context of children's spontaneous activities, as happens typically in the context of the interaction between a mother and her child. In such informal approaches the teacher does not plan in advance the child's language experiences, and may not even consciously formulate language-teaching goals. In contrast, others argue, particularly in the case of culturally disadvantaged children, for a more systematic approach, in which situations or experiences designed to foster particular forms or uses of language are deliberately built into the children's learning environment by their teachers. This distinction between what Cazden (1972) terms the 'more didactic' and 'less didactic' approaches is, of course, only relative, since the provision of any learning environment must involve a certain degree of structuring by teachers, if only because they have to decide what range of activities and materials to provide in school. Nevertheless, this distinction has theoretical and practical importance in the field of teaching disadvantaged children.

Evidence based upon observation and research seems to indicate that a clear statement of aims and objectives and conscious planning by the teacher of children's language experiences are necessary if the language performance of disadvantaged children is to be significantly improved. For example, Thomas (1973) carried out an observational study of twenty children in a nursery class attached to a primary school, in which the language and behaviour of the children, and also of the supervising adults (a teacher and a nursery nurse), during a complete school day were fully recorded. This information was classified and analysed in relation to the children's social class status and their levels of verbal and intellectual ability. No association was found between the use of certain important language forms such as questions, causal explanations and 'if-then' statements, and any of these child factors. In other words, the brighter, verbally more competent children did not show a significantly different pattern of language use in the nursery class setting from their less able peers. Moreover, the adults in the nursery class did not appear to adapt their statements or questions to take account of the differing levels of intellectual and verbal ability of the children. The author suggested that these results reflected a minimal degree of interaction between children and staff, and she concluded that 'traditional' nursery methods of child-initiated and child-directed activity may not promote children's language development. She recommended that greater emphasis should be placed upon the aims of cognitive and linguistic growth at the nursery school stage.

Thomas's conclusions are based upon the study of just one nursery class and should be viewed accordingly, but other writers working in different settings have come to similar conclusions. In the United States, for example, Bereiter and Engelmann (1966) question the relevance, for disadvantaged children, of a school environment which allows the child considerable freedom of choice of activity and which places great emphasis on social contact among children. Such an environment, they argue, ideally complements the middle-class home which is socially more restrictive, and where the child is guided and taught by his parents, whereas it merely replicates the home and neighbourhood of the disadvantaged child in its freedom and scope for social contact.

A prominent feature of British schools compared with, say, American schools is the scope they provide for peer-group talk. Such talk might be thought to aid children's language development, but this does not necessarily follow. As part of his study of the language of five- to seven-year-old children, Bernstein (cited in Cazden, 1972) 'eavesdropped' on conversations taking place between children playing in 'Wendy Houses'. He concluded that the language used in such a setting was of rather a stereotyped kind, consisting of well-rehearsed phrases or responses which did little to extend language development. Similarly, Cazden (1972) listened-in to the peer-group talk of British nursery school children in a Wendy House and, on the basis of such observation, felt that, if contact with adults is lacking, even a rich school environment may do little more to develop the communicative competence of children than informal play situations outside school.

At a more formal level, several attempts have been made to review the effectiveness of compensatory education programmes carried out in the USA for the benefit of disadvantaged children. In one such study, Hawkridge *et al.* (1968) found that the following features clearly distinguished the more successful from the less successful programmes:

(i) careful planning and clear statement of academic objectives;

(ii) the use of small groups and a high degree of individualisation of instruction;

(iii) instruction and materials that were relevant and closely linked to the programme objectives;

(iv) high intensity treatment;

(v) teacher training in the methods of the programme.

Bissell (1968) reviewed a number of research projects carried out in the USA, and suggested that the more effective compensatory programmes had in common a heavy emphasis on language development and teacher-directed activities which structured the children's experiences.

In discussing the apparently greater effectiveness of the more didactic programmes, Cazden (1972) suggests that one important feature of such programmes, as compared with more informal 'child-centred' approaches, is simply that they may guarantee a more equal distribution of teacher attention among children in a class by providing definite times when the teacher and small groups of children can talk together. She also suggests that the more structured programmes convey more clearly to children what kind of talking is valued in school, which is valuable to children from home backgrounds providing limited experience of different language functions. However, she also points out that the gains shown by children receiving language programmes may be relatively specific to the language tests and assessments used in evaluating the programmes and may not, therefore, transfer to other, 'real life' situations.

It does not follow from the above discussion that, in the hands of a highly skilled teacher who is clearly aware of what she wishes to achieve, the 'non-didactic' approach to language development, characteristic of the British infant school, cannot achieve as good, or even better, results than the more systematic programmes. However, for this to happen, the teacher needs to provide a wide range of learning situations in the classroom, and to be fully aware of the potential for language development inherent in these situations. Whenever possible, she, or another competent adult, needs to be present in such situations so as to capitalize on their teaching value. All this requires considerable powers of organization and continual alertness on the part of the teacher, and there is always the danger that the children most in need of help will not spontaneously ask questions or otherwise initiate contact with the teacher, and may not, therefore, receive the attention they need. To avoid this danger it may well be necessary for all teachers to build into the curriculum definite times for more systematic language activities based upon more firmly structured learning situations. The approach adopted by the Programme Development Unit of the present project, whose work is described in the following section, is to accept the 'child-centred' learning orientation of the British infant school, with its emphasis on flexibility and teacher guidance rather than direction. A teachers' handbook was prepared which was designed to help the infant school teacher to clarify her language teaching aims and objectives, and to suggest ways of realizing them through the informal learning situations that normally arise in the infant school. At the same time, associated with the handbook are suggestions for more structured language activities designed to foster specific important language skills. These more formal activities would complement the normal infant school activities and help to reinforce the language learning which takes place in them. The handbook should be regarded as a resource which can be adapted and developed by infant school teachers according to their own inclinations and the needs of their particular children.

A LANGUAGE PROGRAMME FOR DISADVANTAGED INFANT SCHOOL CHILDREN

Rationale

The aim of the Programme Development Unit (PDU) of the Compensatory Education Project was to develop a teaching programme to help culturally deprived children at the infant school stage, with particular emphasis upon the first school year (age range four to six years). The Unit concentrated its efforts on preparing materials for helping the language development of deprived children, because a review of the literature and the findings of another unit of the project (see Chapter 5) pointed to language deficits as the key to poor school development in these children. Moreover, the Unit established a number of teachers' groups from schools serving 'deprived areas', and early discussion with these groups soon showed that the teachers wished to develop materials and methods which foster greater communicative competence in their children. At the same time it was fully realized that the fostering of language should be seen in the context of other educational considerations, in particular those of meeting the social, emotional, creative and imaginative needs of infant school children.

Given the broad aim of devising a language teaching programme, the question arose as to what the specific objectives of the programme should be and what approach to learning it should be based upon. Compensatory programmes can be classified according to the breadth or narrowness of their language teaching objectives. Some programmes such as the Peabody Language Development Kits (Dunn and Smith, 1965) are broad in coverage, embracing, for example, general vocabulary enrichment, the teaching of key sentence patterns (syntax), and the use of language to serve a variety of functions, ranging from logical and mathematical to social and emotional. In contrast, other programmes deal more intensively with a narrower range of teaching objectives (see Chazan and Cox, 1976). For example, the programmes devised by Blank and Solomon (1968 and 1969) and Bereiter and Engelmann (1966) emphasize the teaching of language as a tool for problem solving and for logically ordering, classifying and interrelating experiences. Both pairs of authors believe that the value of broadly-based 'total enrichment' programmes is likely to be limited because they are not based upon diagnosis of the key deficiencies in culturally deprived children. Blank and Solomon (1968 and 1969) consider that the most vital deficiency of such children is their inability to use language as a means of organizing and assimilating their experience, i.e. as a symbolic system for thinking.

The PDU language programme adopts a rationale similar to that of Blank and Solomon in that it focusses upon the vocabulary and language structures associated with logical thinking and reasoning. These 'cognitive' language skills were chosen as objectives in the light of the research findings described in Chapter 5 and also of discussion with the teachers' groups working with the PDU. By focussing on these objectives it is hoped to help disadvantaged children to develop more fully what Bernstein (1971) has called an 'elaborated speech code' which will enable them to cope with the situations in school where a formal style or 'register' of speech is appropriate. Such situations will require, for example, accurate descriptions and explanations, and the use of questions to elicit information. The particular language skills chosen will be described in more detail later in this section, but it should be stressed that the concentration in the PDU programme upon the cognitive aspects of language in no way implies that other functions of language are not equally important in a child's development (see Halliday, 1969, for a useful discussion of these other functions).

On the question of the teaching method adopted in the PDU programme, it is useful to consider the three types of teacher-child or child-child interaction distinguished by Bartlett (1972) in her review of pre-school language programmes. These were called 'pattern repetition', 'instructional dialogue' and 'improvised interaction', respectively. In *pattern repetition* the child is encouraged to imitate the teacher's language model as closely as possible and his success is judged in terms of how accurately he does so. The teacher takes on a highly directive role, presenting the materials, modelling the language patterns, asking questions and providing feedback (see Bereiter and Engelmann, 1966, for a good example of this approach).

In the *instructional dialogue* pattern of teaching the emphasis is upon *discussion* between teacher and child, and the latter's task is not to imitate the teacher's sentences, but to use language to convey and to organize information accurately. The teacher provides the structured learning situations and guides the child's thinking by asking leading questions and making suggestions, but the child has greater freedom of action and response than in the pattern repetition approach, for he can ask his own questions and make his own observations. Blank and Solomon's programme is based upon this teacher style, which also seems to characterize the model of teacher-pupil language interaction advocated by Tough (1977b) for British infant schools.

In the *improvised interaction* pattern of learning the teacher plays a much less prominent role, for the child is put in a situation where he can communicate with others in a variety of different ways. Socio-dramatic play, in which children take on various roles, and communication game situations, in which children have to convey information to each other, are good examples of this type of interaction (see Gahagan and Gahagan, 1970 for further examples of this approach). As in the case of instructional dialogue, the child's success is judged in terms of how accurately and effectively he communicates, and not upon his production of pre-selected language patterns.

Of the above types of learning patterns, the instructional dialogue and improvised interaction styles seem to be most in keeping with the philosophy of the British infant school, since they allow children to respond in individual ways to the learning situations provided. The PDU programme was based upon learning approaches similar to these, and not upon pattern repetition.

Having decided upon the goals and learning methods of the language programme, the PDU still had to decide upon its format. Should it consist of a set of highly structured activities following a strict progression, and accompanied by a detailed script for the teacher to follow, as in the case of the Peabody Kit? Alternatively, should it comprise a set of guidelines and suggested activities which the teacher could select from and adapt as required? As pointed out at the end of the previous section of this chapter, it was decided to adopt the latter, more flexible approach, since this was much more in keeping with the infant school tradition. This decision was fully endorsed by the teachers taking part in the discussion groups. As a result, the output of the PDU took the form of a Teachers' Handbook rather than a detailed, pre-sequenced 'package' of language activities. For some, the term 'language programme' connotes a highly-sequenced and prescriptive set of activities. However, for convenience, the output of the PDU will be referred to as a programme, but it should be realized that the handbook is essentially a *guide* for teachers.

Plan of Teachers' Handbook

Two years' intensive work by the PDU led to the production of the Handbook entitled 'Language Development and the Disadvantaged Child' (Downes, 1978). The experimental version of the 'programme' was tried out in infant schools in a number of education authorities in England and Wales. The purpose of this try-out was to gain the opinion of a body of teachers, other than those involved in the experimental work, of the value of the selected activities and to invite constructive criticism which would enable the Handbook to be improved further. The final version of the Handbook took into account suggestions made by the teachers in the light of their experience of putting the experimental programme into practice.

After a brief introduction explaining the basis on which the selection of language activities was made by the PDU, the Handbook is divided into four parts. Parts 1, 2 and 3 contain practical suggestions for language stimulation in the classroom. Although these suggestions are orientated towards disadvantaged children, it is likely that many of them will apply to infant school children in general. Part 1 defines seven language skills, selected for emphasis in the programme on the basis of research and of discussion in the teachers' groups, and suggests activities relating to these skills. Part 2 looks at two of the 'work areas' commonly found in infant school classrooms and gives detailed suggestions as to how the teacher can exploit the language-teaching opportunities which they provide. Part 3 contains examples of supplementary activities and materials, such as language games, and discusses the use of tape-recorded materials and stories. Part 4 is a check-list of the language skills indentified in the Part 1, which is designed to help the teachers to build up through classroom observation, a systematic picture of the language performance of each child.

In the remainder of this chapter the language skills chosen for emphasis in the Handbook will be described and illustrative examples of activities or materials likely to foster their development will be given. This will be followed by a short illustrative account of how these skills can be developed through activities in the 'work areas' and through language games. Finally, the aim and structure of the checklist will be described briefly.

Developing some basic language skills

Part 1 of the Handbook identifies and focusses upon the following important language skills:

  (i) listening
 (ii) naming
(iii) categorizing
 (iv) describing
  (v) denoting position
 (vi) sequencing
(vii) reasoning.

As already explained, these skills were identified by the teacher groups involved as being particularly important in relation to the educational needs of disadvantaged children. There are, of course, other ways of analysing the language process but the above scheme reflected the priorities of our teachers and also has some support from research. It should be stressed that language is more than an accumulation of separate skills, but in the Handbook each skill is discussed separately, for convenience, so that specific aims and relevant activities can be highlighted. This approach can help the teacher to recognize particular weaknesses in the disadvantaged child's language and to encourage activities which focus upon them. To say this does not imply that each skill can be dealt with in isolation, for there is considerable overlap among the above skills because of the unified nature of spoken language. Such overlap cannot be avoided and should, indeed, be encouraged, since practising one particular aspect of language skill may incidentally strengthen another aspect. The skills will now be discussed in more detail.

(i) *Listening* Many disadvantaged children lived in overcrowded home conditions where there is considerable noise and confusion of sounds, so that little opportunity is given to listen selectively and to develop the listening skills which are so important in the school context. An important goal here is to increase the child's motivation towards listening carefully and selectively, and to discriminate the relevant from the irrelevant. A range of activities and materials is described, in which children will gain systematic practice in discriminating a variety of familiar sounds. For example, common objects, such as an empty jar or piece of paper can be made to produce sounds and children can be invited to listen to them, whilst unable to see their source, and to identify which object is being used to make which sound. Children can also learn to classify objects or materials according to the type of sound they produce.

(ii) *Naming* The focus here is upon a basic 'concrete' vocabulary comprising the names of common objects and actions. A minimal aim is to help the disadvantaged child to acquire and use a vocabulary related to his immediate surroundings and interests. An exhaustive vocabulary list is not provided in the Handbook since much will depend upon the particular classroom setting and the needs and interests of individual children. However, a variety of activities and materials designed to promote a suitable concrete vocabulary is suggested. These include the sorting and identification of common objects, e.g. by touch and feel only, and well-known classroom games such as 'Language Lotto', 'I Spy' and 'Kim's Game' (which involves the naming of missing objects).

78

(iii) *Categorizing*   The literature on disadvantaged children consistently refers to their relative unfamiliarity with, or failure to use, words which classify objects and experiences e.g. people, animals, clothes. Activities and materials are suggested which should help children to understand and use words of this kind, and to learn various criteria for grouping materials. For example, Lotto games have been devised in which various items make up a category (e.g. Animal Lotto, Food Lotto). It is stressed that an important aspect of classifying is the use of the negative, which denotes exclusion from a category. For example, if a child is sorting animals into a group, an item which does not belong, such as a car, can be referred to as '*not* an animal' in this context.

(iv) *Describing*   The disadvantaged child may not understand or use many of those descriptive words or adjectives (of colour, size, texture, etc.) which denote qualities and features of objects. Similarly, adverbs such as 'quickly', 'slowly', 'quietly', which distinguish between actions, may not be used or understood. The main aim of the suggested activities is to encourage the child to discern differences in quality and type between a variety of objects and actions, and to use appropriate words which express these differences, so expanding and extending his language. Various suggestions for activities likely to promote the use of adjectives and adverbs are offered. These include the sorting of objects according to colour, shape, size etc., the use of display tables to illustrate descriptive concepts, such as roundness, and classroom games such as 'Surprise Box', in which a number of familiar objects are placed in a box and the child tries to describe them in terms of feel and texture, i.e. on the basis of handling, but not seeing, the objects. Suggestions are made for basing the learning of important adverbs upon physical games, mime, dramatic and expressive work.

(v) *Denoting position*   As in the case of category words described above, evidence suggests that disadvantaged children may have difficulty in understanding and using words that denote an object's position in relation to its surroundings, e.g. 'under', 'over', 'through', 'behind'. The objective in the activities under this heading is to help children to acquire and use the relatively small number of such positional words. It is suggested that many school and work area activities lend themselves to the learning of these important positional concepts. For example, in physical games, the child may be asked to 'jump *over* the box', 'crawl *through* the hoop' or 'run *around* the chair'.

(vi) *Sequencing* The ability to organize events verbally in sequence is of great importance in communicating stories, instructions, daily events, 'news' and other narratives. Some important aspects of sequencing events include understanding and using the following:

'linking' words of time, such as then, before, after, while; 'sequence' words, such as first, next;
words denoting broad units of time, such as morning, afternoon, today;
a variety of tenses.

The advantaged child has the benefit of hearing, through conversation with his parents, language which is directly associated with daily routines such as getting up, washing, dressing, eating and going to school, e.g. '... wash *before* you get dressed ...', '... You can do that *later*, but first ...'. Not only do daily events such as these follow a pattern, but the key relational words of time are used frequently in a variety of situations. This type of experience enables the child to use these key relational words in a variety of other situations which involve sequencing events.

For the disadvantaged child, on the other hand, not only is his daily routine at home less orderly, but he also lacks the benefit of hearing systematic language patterns associated with these events. It is, therefore, not surprising that the disadvantaged child often has poorly developed ideas of sequence, order and duration of time.

The main objective underlying the activities in this section of the Handbook is to enable the child to understand the key relational words of time in a variety of situations in which sequence is important. For example, a child can be shown a set of three or four pictures, depicting a series of events in a scrambled order, and asked to put them in their correct sequence and tell a short story about them. In time he can be encouraged to attempt longer sequences and to rely less on supporting pictures. The school or classroom daily routine also provide good opportunities for highlighting these important concepts of time and sequence.

(vii) *Reasoning* The term Reasoning is used to refer broadly to the use of language for planning, predicting (anticipating) and solving problems. The advantaged child is accustomed to using language to plan his activities and to think about 'problems'. He will often talk to himself (aloud or subvocally) before and during an activity. In this way he can use language to discuss 'plans' and intentions, consider several alternative courses of action, and make decisions *before* carrying out actions.

This is a crucial area of language usage as it enables the child to plan and explore systematically and purposefully, guided by his own language. The disadvantaged child, on the other hand, who is not accustomed to using language to plan and anticipate events, may play in a haphazard and unsystematic manner. Without an overall verbal 'plan', play and exploration tend to be desultory, and one action is unrelated to another.

Another important aspect of the advantaged child's language is his constant questioning. He frequently demands to know why certain things happen and is constantly searching for cause. By contrast, the disadvantaged child does not appear to have the same curiosity and questioning attitude or the ability to ask questions purposefully and systematically.

The purpose of the activities in this section is to encourage the disadvantaged child to use language to plan activities and talk about his intentions *before* actually carrying them out. In making a simple prediction, 'It will fall', or a plan, 'I'll put the block on the box', he is recalling previous play experiences with similar materials and relating these to present circumstances so that he can anticipate what is likely to happen and plan accordingly.

In encouraging the child to make a prediction or plan, it is important that he should put his statement to the test by carrying out the action. Of course, the action will not always accurately correspond to the statement, but accuracy is less important than the actual verbal attempt to predict and plan. Predicting and planning involve the use of relational words such as 'if', 'because' and 'but', e.g. 'It will break *if* you drop it', 'She is crying *because* she fell'.

Activities which are particularly useful in encouraging the child to *predict* can quite easily be structured by the teacher in the context of normal classroom activities. For example, the child can be provided with a set of common objects, such as a rubber ball, wooden block and a feather, and asked to predict what will happen when they fall, e.g. will they bounce? what sound will they make?

Similarly, suggestions are made for giving children the opportunity to *plan* their activities. For example, in the process of cooking, the ingredients can be named and the successive stages of the process (pouring, mixing, baking, etc.) described in advance.

Simple *problems* are presented in the form of a concrete practical situation, or in pictorial or verbal form, and suggested activities are described in each case. For example, a ball can be placed on top of a cupboard and the children asked to suggest how to get it down. Alternatively, a picture of a suitable scene such as a railway or bus station can be covered by a large sheet of paper in which a hole is cut revealing only a small part of the picture. The position of the hole can be varied and the child can then be asked to speculate what the whole picture portrays, on the basis of several such 'samplings'.

Work areas and language development

Part 1 of the Handbook discusses ways in which language skills can be fostered through a wide variety of school and classroom activities. Part 2 outlines the possibilities for language development that are inherent in specific work areas commonly found in infant schools such as Sand, Water, Home and Music Corners, each of which provides an environment for exploration and discussion.

In organizing and equipping work areas, it is important to provide a variety of topics of interest so that the child can explore and manipulate materials, using important language skills in many different situations. Crucial language skills are learned through understanding and expressing relationships (e.g. of space, time, cause-and-effect) between objects, actions and ideas. Virtually any materials which interest the child can be used to illustrate these types of relationship and stimulate the appropriate language patterns. Since the range of possible approaches is so wide, it is important that the notes on work areas and materials in the Handbook should be regarded only as examples which indicate the potential use of simple materials in fostering language development.

Detailed suggestions for materials and activities are offered for only two work areas, namely 'Sand' and 'Home' Areas, but the teacher can readily adapt these suggestions in relation to any other type of work area. The breakdown of language skills adopted in Part 1 of the Handbook is also used in this section. Some illustrative examples from the Handbook of suggested activities in the Sand Area now follow.

Listening—children can experiment in producing sounds made by various objects, in relation to dry or wet sand, and games can be played in which the teacher or a child creates a sound and another child tries to guess how it was produced, e.g. by sprinkling dry sand on paper, dropping a stone on wet sand, drawing a rod across wet sand.

Denoting position—discussion relating to the movement of sand in pouring and modelling, and the position of objects in the sand tray, can help the child to understand and use positional words, e.g. sand goes *through* the holes in the sieve, the hill is in the *middle* of the tray. Similarly, games involving verbal instructions or descriptions, such as 'Hunt the Treasure', can provide excellent practice in using and understanding positional concepts.

Reasoning—children can be encouraged to predict the results of performing certain operations with objects and sand, e.g. the kind of marks a toy car or rake will make when it is drawn across damp sand, how dry/wet sand will flow out of a funnel.

Similarly, the sand corner provides opportunity for *planning* a variety of buildings such as a tower, fort, rocket or landscape, i.e. the child can be asked to describe the materials he will need for his construction and the steps he will follow in carrying it out. Simple situations which pose practical problems can also be contrived by the teacher quite easily, e.g. asking 'How can you make a sandcastle collapse?' might result in several answers such as '... knock it down with a ...', 'dig away the sand at the bottom' or 'drop something on it'.

Language games

The main aim of the language games described in Part 3 (Chapter 9) of the Handbook is to give children the opportunity to practice the language skills and patterns emphasized in Section A and to encourage purposeful verbal communication between children. The games provide highly structured language situations and, as such, are intended to complement and reinforce the language learning that takes place more informally in the normal range of classroom activities. It is suggested that disadvantaged children would benefit from regular, systematic experience of these games, e.g. the teacher could set aside, say, twenty minutes daily for these activities. The games can also provide a useful means of helping the teacher to check on the child's progress in acquiring language skills. A further advantage of the games is that, provided that they have been suitably introduced and are appropriate to the particular children's level of language skill, they require a minimum of teacher supervision and thus release the teacher for more intensive involvement with children in other contexts. Whenever possible, therefore, the games are designed on a 'self-correcting' basis. At the same time it is stressed that the games should not be used in isolation but as part of an overall approach to helping language development.

Most of the rules and procedures described are based upon well-known games, such as Lotto, and various card games which involve collecting, discarding and exchanging pictures, but the procedures are intended only as examples which can be adapted and added to by the teacher. For example, most of the games can be made more difficult by increasing the number of cards and by introducing more complex pictures which require finer discriminations and more elaborate language patterns. In playing the games the various 'moves' made by the child should be accompanied by appropriate use of language. Before a game can be played satisfactorily, the children should be familiar with the procedure and language involved, and careful guidance by the teacher or aide is necessary in the early stages.

Each game is accompanied by a detailed instruction sheet for the teacher and an indication of which specific language skill it is intended to provide practice in. Appended to this chapter is an example of one of the games designed to give practice in the language skills of describing and denoting position.

Check-list

The purpose of this check-list is to help the teacher to build up a 'profile' of each child's language skills, based largely upon observation during normal classroom activities. It consists of a set of ratings for specific aspects of language use, following the classification of language skills adopted in previous sections of the Handbook. Each rating is on a four-point scale ranging from 'very good' to 'well below average', in relation to the language skills of children in general. Each rating is accompanied by a brief descriptive statement designed to guide the teacher in making her assessment. The following example relates to the language skill of categorizing:

Description	Rating
Uses a variety of category words including, for example, furniture, vegetables, tools, musical instruments	1
Uses commoner category words such as: people, animals, clothes, food	2
Uses few category words	3
Seldom/never uses category words—has little understanding of them	4

In addition, space is provided on the individual rating chart for ratings of clarity of speech, comprehension of instructions and attentiveness to stories. The first assessment of language should be made as soon as practicable after school entry so that the areas of language functioning in which a given child is particularly deficient can be identified and appropriate language activities selected or devised. Subsequent assessments, say towards the end of each term, would help the teacher to keep a simple regular check on each child's progress.

Appendix

INSTRUCTIONS FOR BUILDING GAME

Aim

To give the child practice in naming and describing objects (such as red block, green car and cork) and denoting the position of an object in relation to other objects.

Materials (see illustration)

(a) A set of the following pictures (or models):

Tower—blocks, cork
Tower—block, cotton reels
Tower—large and small blocks
Train—blocks, cork
Bridge—blocks, cardboard, car, cork
Bridge/crane—blocks, pencil, car, string
Ramp—blocks, cardboard strip
House—blocks, cardboard

(b) Toy cars and lorries
Blocks of various colours
Corks, cotton reels, strips of cardboard, piece of string (with loops at each end).

Players

Two.

Procedure

Two players A and B are seated opposite eacn other. A has the set of pictures arranged in a pack and placed face downward in front of him, and B has the materials. The players are told that A will tell B how to make a 'building'. They can ask and answer questions but they must not point.

B moves all his toys to one side (they can be placed in an open box or tray), leaving a clear area in front of him. A picks up the first card and holds it *so that B cannot see the pictures*. A cardboard screen can be placed between the two players so they cannot see each other's picture or materials. A then gives instructions such as:

'Take the yellow block and the green block ... put the green block on the yellow block ... put the cork on the green block.'

After B has assembled the tower, both players can check to see if the model is the same as A's picture. The players can then change places and repeat the procedure—this time B instructs and A builds. The procedure is repeated using the next card and so on.

tower—blocks, cork

tower—block, reel

train

bridge

Cards used for Building Game

87

7

Bilingual Children

There has been a steady decrease in the use of the Welsh language during this century, and this has often been accompanied by a decline in the population of the areas in which it has survived. Thus, a disadvantaged child who was also Welsh-speaking would not only labour under handicaps similar to those of his English-speaking counterpart, but would face the additional difficulties inherent in his being a member of a dwindling minority. His deficiencies in language development would be further complicated by the presence in his community, and in his home via radio and television, of another language of world prestige.

The Welsh Language Unit (WLU) was therefore set up as part of the project in order to study the linguistic development of disadvantaged Welsh-speaking children in the infant school, their adjustment to the school situation, and the effect of social disadvantage on their educational attainments.

DESIGN OF ENQUIRY

Two groups of first-language-Welsh children, one having a 'deprived' home background (the Dep group) and the other 'non-deprived' (the Con group), were matched for age, sex, school and teacher, date of school entry, non-verbal intelligence and Welsh linguistic background. (Subsequent testing revealed a difference between the two groups in non-verbal intelligence, but this was allowed for in the statistical analysis of the results.) Hypotheses were formulated that

   (i) the language of the 'deprived' (Dep) group, in both Welsh and English, would be less well-developed at 5 + years than the control (Con) group;

  (ii) the language of the Dep group, in both Welsh and English would continue to be less well-developed at the age of 7 + years than the Con group; and that

 (iii) the Dep group would be less well-adjusted to school and

would have made less educational progress at the age of 7 +
years than the Con group.

Thirty-two pairs of children (in all, 28 boys and 36 girls), in eighteen
schools, formed the final sample. Selection of children for each group
was based on the number of pointers to deprivation revealed by a 'Social
Disadvantage Index' which was completed for each child by his
headteacher, and on recommendations made by the class teachers. It
must be remembered that the term 'deprived' was used in a relative
sense only, i.e. the Dep group was more deprived, on the basis of the
Disadvantage Index, than the Con group. In fact, it proved difficult
to obtain two groups widely differing on criteria of deprivation, because of the general interest in the well-being of their children shown
by the parents in the areas selected for testing.

There were, however, several significant differences between the two
groups in the final sample. The Con children had a richer pre-school
experiential background, they showed more liking for school, and
their parents were more likely to co-operate with the school. There
was a strong middle-class element among the Con parents, the Dep
parents being mainly manual workers. More Dep children were in
receipt of free meals, they showed a greater incidence of listlessness
and fatigue in school, and their families were more likely to have
problems or difficulties.

The schools which the children attended were situated in South
Wales, either in rural surroundings or in semi-rural areas with some
industrialization, mainly coal-mining. According to the 1961 Census
data, the majority of the population was bilingual, and the schools
taught mainly through the medium of Welsh, though this policy was
carried out in a variety of ways and with varying degrees of bilin-
gualism. Some schools taught mathematics in Welsh, some in English,
and others used both languages when teaching this subject. All the
children began learning to read in Welsh. In thirteen schools they were
then introduced to English reading, usually during their final infant
school year, while in the other five schools, English reading was not
introduced until entry into the junior department.

The extent to which the English language was used in other activities varied considerably. Of the 18 schools, three followed a bilingual policy and English was introduced into most activities throughout the day; nine schools used English to a lesser extent; and in the remaining six schools, little or no English was used and the medium of instruction was almost exclusively Welsh.

LANGUAGE TESTING

1. *At 5+ years*

The majority of the sample had already spent approximately a year at school when tested, during 1969, at the age of 5 + years. The general scarcity of standardized Welsh tests made it necessary for tests of oral proficiency in the Welsh language to be specially devised, an attempt being made to parallel the English tests used. The children were tested individually in both languages, in

1. receptive (or listening) vocabulary
2. productive (or spoken) vocabulary
3. oral comprehension
4. grammatical rules and morphology.

The children's articulation, tempo and vocabulary in spoken Welsh and English were assessed by their class teachers, who also completed five schedules for each child over a period of $2\frac{1}{2}$ years. These schedules gave information not only on progress in the basic skills, but also on other aspects of child development, including adjustment to school, social and emotional adjustment and social competence.

The results of the oral proficiency test battery and the teachers' ratings showed that, at the age of 5 + years, the Con children were more adaptable to the school situation, were making a better response to schooling, and were significantly superior to the Dep children in language development in both Welsh and English. The first hypothesis was therefore supported.

However, the children's responses to test items and the comments of some teachers implied a low standard of spoken Welsh in many members of both Con and Dep groups. One headteacher remarked, 'The majority of these children speak a pidgin Welsh and English on entry. They don't speak one language properly.'

90

The investigation also showed that the children were bilingual, in the sense of being able to understand and speak both Welsh and English; but a detailed comparison of their performance in each language could not be made because of lack of suitable test materials. However, test results and teachers' ratings tentatively suggested that the gap between the two groups in language development was greater in Welsh than in English, so that the Dep group would not be at such a disadvantage in English as in Welsh.

As might be expected, the average score of both groups in the English tests was lower than that of a monolingual English population. It was also found that the average performance in spoken English was lower than in receptive (or listening) vocabulary, probably because the children's use of the language was limited and their main contact with English was in the passive role of the listener. A Dep child who performed well in one language, in relation to the rest of his group, was likely to do equally well in the other. This was true, but to a lesser extent, of the Con group also. Finally, teachers' ratings showed that the Dep group was less able to comprehend the teacher's Welsh language than the Con group.

2. At 7 + years

The same tests were re-administered at 7 + years, with the exception of the tests of oral comprehension. In addition, two tests, which required responses in the form of sentences, were given in both languages.

The results of the Welsh language tests showed that the differences between the two groups had remained at the same highly significant level, but there was no evidence that the gap between them had widened. Teachers' ratings also showed the Con group to be superior in several aspects of the Welsh language, e.g. fluency, comprehension, tempo, articulation and range of vocabulary. The second hypothesis was therefore supported as far as the Welsh language was concerned, i.e. that the Con group would be superior to the Dep in language development at 7 + years.

In English, the hypothesis was only supported in some aspects of the language. The difference between the two groups in receptive vocabulary remained at the same highly significant level as at 5 + years, but the difference had lessened in two other tests, suggesting that the gap in English language development had narrowed slightly. In two tests involving grammatical rules and sentence construction, the differences were not significant. The overall picture, therefore, showed less difference between the two groups in English than in Welsh, as had already been shown at 5 + years. Moreover, performance in the standardized English tests showed considerable improvement in both groups, the average test age having increased by two years in one test. It seems, therefore, that with relatively little English being spoken at home or in school, both groups had made considerable progress in this language, though verbalizing still lagged behind receptive vocabulary, as had been the case at 5 + years.

This difficulty in verbalizing was present in both languages, as evidenced by the reticence of the children in tests requiring the production of sentences. Many were hesitant and slow to respond, and the majority gave very brief replies. In the Welsh tests, this reticence seemed to be caused by a disinclination to reveal the shortcomings in their vocabulary. When they realized that there was no disapproval if they used English words, most of them replied more promptly.

The somewhat low general standard of spoken Welsh implied in the 5 + results was verified. Deficiencies in certain areas of language were common to both groups, though they were more pronounced among the Deps, and consisted of the intrusion of English terminology, and inaccuracies of syntax, gender, mutation and other morphological structures. In the English test responses, the only linguistic interference occurred in the vocabulary tests, when certain words were known only in Welsh. There was considerably more linguistic interference in the Welsh test responses, probably caused by the dominance of the English language in the country as a whole.

The children varied considerably in their mastery of both languages. In some districts, they were extremely hesitant in speaking English and were obviously far more fluent in Welsh despite its English intrusions; in other areas, the children seemed equally at ease in either language; and in yet other places they seemed happier speaking in English. However, correlations between the English and Welsh test results showed that, on the whole, a good performance in one language, in relation to the rest of the group, tended to accompany a similar performance in the other.

92

Teachers' ratings showed that at 7 + years, the Dep group had a significantly higher incidence of behavioural disorders than the Con group, though in overall emotional adjustment the gap between them had narrowed slightly. Thus, although the first part of hypothesis 3 was supported, i.e. that the Dep children would be less well-adjusted to school at 7 + years, the earlier difference between the groups in this respect had lessened slightly by the end of their infant school career. This says much for the quality of the teaching the children had received. The teachers showed interest in, and concern for, them all, and nowhere was there evidence of prejudice against deprived children, such as has been mentioned in the American literature.

EDUCATIONAL PROGRESS

As might be expected, the differences between the two groups in adjustment to school and in language development, affected the performance of the children in school activities, and the second part of hypothesis 3, that the Dep group would have made less educational progress than the Con group by 7 + years, was also supported. Teachers' ratings had shown a highly significant difference between the attainments of the two groups in the basic subjects throughout their infant schooling, and this was confirmed by the test battery administered at 7 + years, during the summer term of 1971. Tests of reading comprehension, word recognition, spelling and free writing were given in both languages, as well as a test in basic mathematics.

The Con group was superior to the Dep in both the reasoning and the mechanical processes of mathematics, in spelling and in word recognition. The children were under a far greater disadvantage in the test of English free writing than in the corresponding Welsh test, because many had never previously written in English in school. Nevertheless, the average word count was similar in both languages in the Con group, while in the Dep group the average score was higher in English. Moreover, the difference between the two groups in reading comprehension was less in English than in Welsh, and in range of written vocabulary (in the 'free writing' tests) was not significant in

93

English, though significant at the 5 per cent level in Welsh. All this implies that the gap between the two groups in some aspects of reading and writing was narrower in English than in Welsh.

Earlier evidence of a somewhat low standard of spoken Welsh was reflected in the free writing tests. The same errors occurred as in the oral language tests, and also evident was incorrect use of tenses and conjugation of verbs. There was a constant use of the continuous past tense when the simple past tense would have been more appropriate. In the use of the simple past tense, the children of both groups were more proficient in English, the superiority in English being particularly marked in the Dep group.

There was also a strong tendency in the whole sample for ability in reading, and to a lesser extent writing, in one language to be accompanied by a similar ability in the other language when compared with the rest of the group. This tendency for ability in one language to accompany a like ability in the other had also been noticeable in the oral language test results at $5+$ and $7+$ years. It seems erroneous, therefore, to assume that a knowledge of English necessarily has an adverse effect on Welsh, and that there has to be a monolingual approach in infant schools in order to safeguard the Welsh language.

CONCLUSION

The Gittins Report (1967) states that '... the real problem of teaching Welsh lies, at present, not in the Welsh-speaking areas but in those schools which teach Welsh as a second language ...' (p. 247). It may be that, as a result of this belief, we have concentrated too much of our resources on the teaching of Welsh as a second language, and given insufficient attention to the education of children in Welsh-medium schools.

It has been found, with reference to infant school immigrants, that the 'language bath' method is not always as efficacious as it seems. Some children 'switch off', while others acquire a language for social purposes which conceals gaps in their linguistic ability. It seems that a similar situation existed with some children in this sample. It was apparent that English had remained their dominant language at $7+$ years, after a considerable period of schooling in Welsh.

The teacher's task was, therefore, extremely difficult, especially if the policy of her school was to exclude the English language as a medium of instruction. She was exhorted by the Gittins Report to 'present a good model of speech', which might not be wholly understood by some of the children, who would then have to cope with three language systems in their environment—English, their 'home' Welsh and their 'school' Welsh.

Throughout their infant school careers, the Dep children were consistently rated as showing less comprehension of the teacher's Welsh language than the Con group. A disadvantaged child has difficulties to overcome which do not face his more fortunate classmates. They affect his adjustment to school and his performance in school activities. Any assets he possesses should, therefore, be exploited to the full. It may well be that his performance in the school situation could be improved if his potential in the English, as well as in the Welsh, language were developed in a bilingual approach. It is true that, as the Gittins Report (p. 246) states, 'the particular linguistic needs of each locality must be carefully ascertained', but with this approach the particular needs of each individual will also be met.

8

Parental Involvement in Education

Despite the evidence in recent educational research in this country and abroad, showing the importance of parental attitudes for a child's educational progress, and despite the apparent increase of parental interest in education as reflected in the growth of such organizations as A.C.E. (the Advisory Centre for Education), C.A.S.E. (Confederation for the Advancement of State Education), the National Federation of Parent-Teacher Associations and the Home-School Council, the subject of parental involvement in education remains somewhat peripheral in much educational literature and in some teacher-training courses.

The research undertaken for the Plowden Committee (1967) showed that a large number of parents would like to know more about how their children learn in school, and also that parental attitudes to education accounted for more of the variation in school achievement than either home circumstances or factors in the school.

The work undertaken by the project provided the opportunity to interview a number of parents from differing types of area and to seek, in the course of this interview, their views on the existing links with their child's infant school and their opinions on various alternative or additional means of contact. In addition, the views of both class and headteachers on similar issues were obtained. This chapter will give the general picture of teachers' and parents' responses to these questions and look at some of the differences between different types of areas.

Two groups of parents were visited when their children were in their second or third year at the infant school. The first group was a sample of 120 parents living in urban areas: 30 from middle class (MC) areas, 30 from settled working class (SWC) areas, and 60 from deprived areas. The second group consisted of all the parents of the 60 children from the rural schools in the project. The response rate was extremely high, all 60 rural parents being interviewed and 116 of the intended 120 in urban areas.

In all of the schools taking part in this research project, there were already formal or informal opportunities for parent-teacher contact. The emphasis, particularly in 'infant only' schools, was on the less formal type of contact when parents brought or collected children or when parents came to discuss some particular problem with the head-teacher or class teacher. Although a few schools had successful Parent–Teacher Associations (often combined with a Junior Department), in general these were viewed with suspicion by headteachers who felt that they were 'run by teachers', or led to parents wanting to have too much control over school activities, or else became social gatherings for a small clique of parents only. Particularly in the deprived areas, headteachers preferred the school to be 'like a club' or 'an open house' for parents to visit at any time. Most schools invited parents, at least occasionally, to events such as plays, concerts or Open Days, though it was unfortunate that in a few cases headteachers felt that they had insufficient accommodation to do this. A small number of schools invited parents to more 'everyday' activities, such as assemblies, or to watch the ordinary classroom routine in progress. One DA head-teacher invited every parent for an individual interview each term.

Fewer than half the schools had attempted any sort of general educational meeting for parents, and few of these had felt them really worthwhile or had good attendances.

In urban schools evening activities were seldom arranged, teachers often living at considerable distances from the school. Rural schools more often arranged evening activities, and many of the teachers in rural schools were part of the local community, meeting parents at other social functions.

Headteachers were asked for their views on the general helpfulness of their pupils' parents. The percentages said to be willing to be of help in school activities varied from 5 to 100, with generally lower figures quoted by the heads of DA schools.

Although all headteachers believed that there were ample opportunities for parents to discuss their children's progress or other matters, only about 25 per cent of parents were said to avail themselves of these opportunities. Headteachers of both DA and SWC schools felt that parents often made enquiries about their child's progress 'incidentally' at other functions, rather than coming specifically to do so.

Few teachers had visited the homes of their pupils. It was felt by most urban teachers to be a measure resorted to only in cases of emergency or illness and one that would not be welcomed by many parents. Most either said that they would be reluctant to do so or positively disagreed with home visits. This reluctance was not so apparent in rural areas where parents were often also encouraged to visit teachers in their own homes. Many teachers were equally dubious about allowing parents actually to help in the classroom setting.

Teachers were asked to rate the general level of parental interest in the children's school progress. Here there was a notable difference between the DA schools and the remainder. Only one DA school rated the parents as having 'very positive interest', while the only five teachers who gave the rating 'little evidence of interest' were in DA schools. Few headteachers felt that parents were actually hostile to the school (though rather more fathers than mothers had an attitude of hostility attributed to them); they thought rather that there was a general indifference or apathy. Teachers were often critical of the ways in which parents tried to help their children with school work, though only three had attempted to give parents any guidance in this. Apart perhaps from hearing their children read to them, parental help in teaching the children was seldom encouraged and often discouraged.

Infant teachers very rarely sought help from outside the school, from welfare officers or social work agencies, in making the necessary links with the home.

THE PARENTS' VIEWS

With very few exceptions, the parents who were visited co-operated willingly in answering a fairly lengthy questionnaire. This good response rate and the degree of interest shown, with the interviewer often being asked almost as many questions as she asked herself, indicates the parents' concern and wish to widen their knowledge of their children's schooling. Several parents expressed appreciation that someone was taking the trouble to ask for their views.

Most parents said that they were interested to learn about the general educational methods used in their children's schools (particularly where these differed dramatically from their own recollected schooldays) and about their own children's progress. When asked about the methods of teaching, very few parents gave the impression that they had an adequate knowledge, particularly of the 'new mathematics' approach or the 'initial teaching alphabet' used in a few schools. This lack of knowledge was much more marked among parents in more deprived areas. This cannot be explained only by differences in opportunities provided by the schools, since a comparison of parents from the 'most deprived' backgrounds with those from the 'least deprived' backgrounds *within* school areas, showed that those from the 'most deprived' backgrounds knew least about teaching methods. This may well indicate less communication between parent and child about school activities in these very deprived homes. These parents also more often felt that these matters should be left to the school and so did not want to know more.

Most parents favoured informal chats with the class teacher as the most helpful way of finding out about what their children did at school, but they also learned from Open Days, from seeing their child's work when it was brought home and in conversation with the child.

Although most parents agreed with the teachers' view that parents could go to the school at any time, many were reluctant to use this opportunity. They often felt that it was not right to 'bother' the teachers unless there was some particularly urgent problem to be discussed. Parental comments such as: 'You can go at other times (besides Open Day) but the teachers are so busy—you don't like to bother them', or 'I've felt that I haven't really needed to go because she seems to be getting on well', or 'I don't like to go because it upsets the child if she thinks I am making a fuss', illustrate this attitude.

Several parents would have appreciated a definite invitation to go to talk to the teacher about their own child's progress, though a few feared that they would feel 'tongue-tied' in this rather 'artificial' situation. A small number favoured written reports on the children's progress. Some felt that, when asked about the child's progress, teachers tended to 'gloss over' difficulties.

Since both formal or informal opportunities for contact with the school were almost always during school hours, few fathers were able to visit the school or meet the teachers. About a quarter of the mothers interviewed said that their husbands felt that it was up to them (the mothers) to make any necessary contacts and then 'report back' to them, particularly at the infant stage. However, about a third of the mothers felt that their husbands would appreciate the opportunity to meet teachers during the evenings.

Most parents, rather naturally, were more concerned to learn about their own children's progress and problems than they were to learn about educational matters in general. However, this did not reflect an unwillingness to help in general activities. While some parents had practical difficulties in offering day-time help, most were keen or willing to help, if they were asked. They were asked for suggestions as to ways in which they thought they might be able to help, and the answers given covered a wide range of activities. Offers made included help in erecting shelving for books, reading to a class while a teacher gave extra help to the more backward children, listening to children reading and helping with parties, outings or sports days. Several parents felt that if they were to help in the classroom it would be preferable *not* to be with their own children.

Parents were asked for their views on teachers visiting them at home. The majority of parents said they would be quite willing for teachers to visit, but several said that this would be putting an un-necessary burden on teachers, who should not be expected to take on this extra task.

CONCLUSION

The questions to both parents and teachers concerning home-school links provoked a great deal of interest and some revealing comments. The overall impression gained was that there is a great deal of goodwill towards the infant schools on the part of parents, a faith in the capa-bility and effectiveness of the teachers and a willingness to help the school or their own children in any way possible. Whilst some parents, it is true, are happy to leave the whole task of education, and even discipline, to the school, many are keen both to learn more about the school's methods and to help and co-operate more than they do at present.

In several ways the responses of the 'most deprived' group were different from those of the others. They were more inclined to feel that they could or should leave the child's education entirely to the school; they more often favoured informal contact with teachers with no 'appointment' system; and the child's father was less likely to take much interest in the schooling, particularly at this early stage. This group of parents also had somewhat lower aspirations for their children's later education, though this should not be taken to imply that they were not keen for their children to do well in learning the more basic skills.

In rural areas, parents and teachers were more likely to be part of a small community and hence meet informally. As parents had often attended the same school as their child, they felt that they knew it well. However, since many pupils were taken to school by bus, parents missed the opportunity of meeting teachers when they took or collected their children.

The Plowden report (1967) states that '... one of the essentials for educational advance is a closer partnership between the two parties to every child's education'. It would seem that there are some parents and, regrettably, still a small number of teachers who need to be convinced that there *are* 'two parties to every child's education'. In one sense, any and every sort of contact between parents and teachers should increase the awareness of this partnership. Little evaluation has been undertaken of the feasibility or effectiveness of different methods of improving home-school contacts, except on a one-school-only basis, but the results of this survey do suggest what parents find most helpful and what further opportunities they would like for contact or involvement.

Parents, on the whole, prefer informal contact with the children's class teachers and, while only a small number felt unwelcome in the school, many were hesitant about approaching teachers, except at times when some problem had arisen, and a few felt that they did not get an honest assessment of the child's behaviour and progress. Many fathers would like the opportunity to attend school functions and meet teachers in the evening.

On the whole, parents are willing to contribute much more help to the school than they are generally asked for. In most cases they wait for the school to take the initiative in asking for help. In the most deprived areas there may well be more who would be reluctant to give help or whose commitments at home or work would make it difficult for them to offer assistance.

The greatest difficulties in forging closer links between the home and the school probably exist at the extreme ends of the social class spectrum. Teachers may well feel threatened by the more articulate and educated professional parent who has very high scholastic aspirations for his or her child and knows, sometimes almost too well, his rights as a parent. At the other end of the scale, the teacher can be discouraged by the apparent apathy and lack of understanding of the purposes of modern education of parents whose own educational level was low and who are sometimes overwhelmed by the problems of coping with large families, low income, overcrowded conditions in the home, and other social or emotional problems. Any bridging of the gap between home and school in this latter case will depend largely on the initiative being taken by the school. On the whole, the survey suggests that home visits by teachers would not be unwelcome, particularly if these were known not to be restricted to instances of problem behaviour or backwardness.

Undoubtedly there are a few parents so completely overwhelmed by the problems of coping at a minimal level with a home and family that they can offer little to the child or school to ease the burden on the teacher. However, even in the deprived areas of this study, there are large numbers of parents who are keen to do anything to help their own child or the school, and it would seem a pity if some effort were not made to utilize this voluntary help to the full.

9

Overview

This last chapter surveys the work that the project has accomplished. It begins by reviewing the principles on which the project was based, in order to assess their validity today. It then examines the implications of the project's work for teachers, including some of the research findings that deserve mention. The chapter concludes with a proposal for future developments.

The choice of the infant school

This project, as its title indicates, was set firmly in the infant school; indeed it is to the infant school teacher that this book is primarily addressed. The decision to place a compensatory education project at this stage of the education process was taken very early in the formulation of the proposals for the project. At that time, the middle 1960's, the bulk of educational research and development was concerned with children in the primary and secondary stages of education. To a large extent, curricular materials were prepared to meet the needs of the older pupil. Studies of children's emotional and social development tended to concentrate on the problems of the middle years of childhood and of adolescence. Since then the tide of interest and research has washed into the pre-school years. The emphasis which the Government White Paper (Department of Education and Science, 1972)* placed on the development of pre-school education was a political response to this educational concern for the very young. But the infant school has been left relatively undisturbed. There has been no work on the infant school as important as that begun by Dorothy Gardner in the 1940's, for example (Gardner, 1950).

Securely based on the principles of the child-centred movement, the infant schools have proceeded to develop teaching methods, to improve skills and to foster an atmosphere that has been the envy of educationists from many parts of the world. Perhaps for this reason, re-

---

* *Education: A Framework for Expansion* (Command 5174). London: HMSO.

search workers have left them well alone. Infant schools may not be deprived, but they have certainly been neglected.

It seemed in 1965, when the first proposal for this project was being drafted, that the infant school was a key point in compensatory education policy. There were two reasons for this, the first of which was a pragmatic one.

The evidence of the 1960's suggested that the very early years of childhood—indeed the first year or two of life—held the key to successful intervention with deprived children. Later work has tended to support this view. Nevertheless it seemed to us, on practical grounds, most unlikely that economic resources would be available to provide for all very young children in need. The problem is one of delivering resources to children when they are part of scattered family units before the start of school. For this reason it seemed that the infant school, when for the first time all children meet an organized educational influence, was the critical point for large-scale intervention to be feasible. The infant school does not cover the earliest years of childhood, but it does cover the earliest years of sustained education for all.

The second reason for setting the project in the infant school was based on research findings. Even if programmes of compensatory education were introduced for pre-school children in the United Kingdom, this by no means removed the important part which the infant school might be expected to play. Even in the 1960's the gains which pre-school projects had claimed for their children were, in many cases, already being shown to be eroded in the first years of formal education. Many workers saw this as an argument against the introduction of early pre-school compensatory education projects. We saw it otherwise as a need to investigate the ways in which any early gains could be sustained and increased across the first years of formal education, rather than being allowed to diminish and die.

For both these reasons the infant school appeared to be the key point in any attempt to improve the development of children growing up in deprived areas.

In retrospect, these views still seem sound. What has arguably been the most successful American experiment in compensatory education, the Milwaukee project (see Page, 1972), has also been one of the most expensive, with an adult-child ratio as low as 1:1 in the first year of life. There has not been any major national diversion of resources to young deprived children on a scale that would enable support of that generosity to be widely available. Newer research has confirmed that immediate gains from less intensive pre-school projects do drop in the first years of compulsory education. The infant school remains potentially a very important sector through which to channel resources for compensatory education and to study the effects of different education strategies.

Deprivation and compensation

The project was concerned, as the title again indicates, with deprivation. At the time the project was conceived, deprivation was seen in the North American sense as a problem which belonged largely to the centres of the great conurbations. The North American projects are largely set in cities like New York and Chicago, Milwaukee and Philadelphia. The project team felt that this was a narrow concept of deprivation. With a loyalty to the education system of Wales as well as England, the team wanted to consider the special problems of children growing up in those areas which constitute the geographical mass of the principality, the rural areas. It seemed that the child on the remote farm might be quite as deprived as the child in the centre of the large city. So our studies included children from this kind of background.

The Welsh context mentioned above brought us face to face with another issue, that of children who were bilingual. It was forcefully argued that the child who had to learn two languages was a child whose experience in any one language would be limited and who might need extra help for this reason. Consequently, as the introduction indicated, the project widened the idea of deprivation by including a special study of the problems of bilingual children.

This leads directly to an attempt to clarify the meaning of terms such as 'deprived child' and 'compensatory education'. When the project started the lack of clear definitions posed a problem. The research units set up their groups of children for study by following the practice of other investigations in this country and abroad. They first turned to areas, deprived according to criteria similar to those established by the Plowden Committee (Department of Education and Science, 1967). The Programme Development Unit worked in the same way.

The Identification Unit was in a different position. Following the child-centred approach that Chapter 1 outlined, it set itself the task of identifying individual children at risk. As the work progressed, it seemed reasonable to consider deprived children needing compensatory education as children whose educational performance deteriorated, where the deterioration was not solely or mainly associated with the handicapping conditions of special education (such as partial hearing or maladjustment) but *was* associated with growing up in a restricted environment. This operational approach to deprivation and compensation still seems a reasonable line to have taken. Chapter 2 (pp. 18–19) gives the characteristics of the four main groups of children 'at risk' which emerged when the data of the enquiry were analysed objectively. It is tempting to allocate descriptions to each of the groups, describing Group A as slow learners, Group B and C as different kinds of deprived children and Group D as maladjusted. But this is to oversimplify the characteristics of the groups which our analysis revealed. Teachers and others interested in these four 'special care' groups defined in this pragmatic way, should read the Swansea Evaluation Profile Handbook (Evans *et al.*, 1978) and the Technical Manual (Evans, 1978).

The research base

Within this context the project has achieved its main aims, which are to provide techniques for the more accurate identification of children at risk at the start of the infant school and to provide teaching materials for enabling the infant teacher to meet the children's educational needs, both techniques and methods beings research-based. Before discussing the implications for teachers of the techniques and materials, the principle of a research-based project needs discussion. From the start, it seemed quite wrong to try to offer identification techniques and teaching materials—diagnosis and treatment—in isolation from research and development. This implied a long time-scale for the project. It is easy to identify children who show problems at the start of the infant school. But these are not necessarily in need of compensatory education. There is a difference between needing compensatory education and showing a developmental lag. Compensatory education should, following the discussion above, compensate children for experiences which would otherwise lead to a gradual deterioration of their attainments relative to others, over the period of their education. The relative deterioration occurs in association with adverse social circumstances. So in order to make identification sensible we had in this project to identify, at five years of age, those children who at a later date would have shown a relative deterioration in their educational growth. The later date was arbitrarily set at the end of the infant school period, which thus gave a maximum three-year period across which experiments on the prediction of later development could take place. This gave the opportunity to build on a base of data which could be reported to users of the project's products.

In the rush to produce methods for identifying children at risk, many investigators omitted to provide data about even the reliability and validity of their material. The survey by Evans and Ferguson (1974) shows the poor theoretical basis of many of the tests and techniques which are now being advocated for identifying 'children at risk'. The profiles which this project has provided have limitations—but at least the users have some idea of their extent.

The same point applied to the development of materials for use with deprived children in this country. The major deficits of children at risk lay in areas which had to be determined. How those deficits changed across the period of an infant school had to be investigated. With this research backing it is possible to devise a programme, or at least suggest the beginnings of a programme, which can be used in infant school work. But the effectiveness of the programme rests on questions such as its acceptability by infant school teachers and its suitability for use in the classroom. For this reason it was essential to set up groups of infant school teachers with experience of deprived children in order to develop and work on the ideas which came to the programme development unit from the central research units of the project.

In retrospect, the links between the research and the development sides of the project were very important, especially for the production of the teaching materials which came from the Programme Development Unit. The findings of the research unit pointed clearly to the prime significance of language deficits, as has been the case for children in the United States. It is no coincidence that the research units found that it was in the area of language and related skills that deprivation had the greatest effect; that measures of language skills figure prominently in the profiles developed by the Identification Techniques

Unit and that the Programme Development Unit concentrated exclusively on language. There could have been some improvement in the articulation of the work of the research and the development units. The programme development unit was phased to start one year behind the research units, to allow for the feed in of information from them. This year's lag was valuable: a lag of two years would have been more effective. This problem was acknowledged and regretted at the planning stage, when it was clear that funding arrangements to cover a longer period could not be guaranteed. But although the detail of the arrangements may not be perfect, the principle of a curriculum development project with a strong research base seems as right now as it did then.

The child-centred principle

Finally, the emphasis of the project was on the individual needs of children rather than on the concept of priority areas (Ferguson *et al.*, 1971). As Chapters 3, 4 and 5 of this book indicate, the variation of children's characteristics within social classes is quite as important as the variation between social classes. In other words there are many children from social classes 4 and 5 whose work improves: there are many children from social classes 1 and 2 whose work deteriorates. From the point of view of the project our concern is with the children, and not their social class background, whatever that may mean.

This is one of the major points of the project and one which the introduction rightly stressed. It is nevertheless worth stressing again that this project took the needs of individual children as its guiding principle. Although the report of the Plowden Committee argued for identifying and providing resources for educational priority areas, this approach has not been wholeheartedly supported by later work (e.g. Ferguson *et al.*, 1971, Barnes, 1975). This emphasis on individual children leads directly to the second section of this overview, which is concerned with implications of the project for teachers.

THE IMPLICATIONS FOR TEACHERS

Screening children

The Identification Techniques Unit has developed the Swansea Evaluation Profile, which is an instrument for screening the children who enter infant schools. Unlike many other instruments, the Profile did not rely solely on the use of tests of child development. The teacher's impression of the child's adjustment to the school situation has been shown to be an important predictor of his progress across the infant school years. So too has been the information which the Head gains of a few salient characteristics of the child's environment. In other words the Profile assesses information of three different sorts—aspects of child development, of school adjustment and of home background. The infant teacher may be interested but not surprised to learn that the medical characteristics of the children did not prove as effective for indicating poor school progress. This point indicates one difference between compensatory and special education. For special education it is essential to measure and assess medical condition. For compensatory education medical condition is not often of prime importance.

Another point about the development of the identification techniques is the way in which they brought together the headteacher and the parent. During the pilot phase, when the unit team was holding briefing meetings with the headteachers of those schools which were helping to try out the parental section of the questionnaire, several headteachers expressed some unease about asking what they felt might be regarded as somewhat personal questions. Others in the groups reassured them and were later vindicated. In fact, one of the interesting pieces of feedback received at later meetings was the extent to which headteachers felt they knew their parents better after having completed the home background section of the questionnaire for all their intake. Several of them found that the need to answer the questions of the profiles started a relationship with some parents which was in itself helpful for the school's understanding of the children, quite apart from the information gained.

Chapter 2 sets out in detail the ways in which the Profile can be used. From the point of view of the class teacher in the infant school two of the five uses outlined in Chapter 2 deserve stressing. First (Use

1, page 16), the Profile provides a means of recording an assessment of school entrants in the three critical areas of development, of home background and of adjustment to school which are mentioned above. This alone is helpful to the teacher even if the profile is put to no further use. But in addition the profile provides information on the extent to which each child's characteristics are unusual in each of these three areas (Use 4, pp. 20–21). This again is valuable since it enables infant school teachers to understand children's behaviour and learning and to take steps to help. It is worth noting, incidentally, that this screening process takes place at least two critical years before the 7 + stage at which the Bullock Committee recommended screening (Department of Education and Science, 1975), albeit with somewhat different objectives.

Profiles also permit children to be allocated to groups with particular kinds of needs (Use 2, pp. 17–19). This is a procedure which may be more useful for Headteachers than class teachers.

Much unease has been generated by the system of designating 'EPA schools'. A coarse classification always leads to inequities, particularly at the borderline, where in this case the EPA label leads to a significant increase in resources. There is, too, a sense in which this system is recreating among schools some of those dangers of divisiveness and labelling which it was set up to alleviate among children. The case for a more flexible estimate of the needs of schools, rather than a rigid EPA/non-EPA label is a strong one. And since the needs of schools are in no small measure the needs of their children, an estimate of the extent of the difficulties in the intake of children should be a reasonable estimate of a school's need for extra resources. Use 3 (p. 20) is helpful here. Extra teaching staff and teaching aides, remedial and language specialists, school social workers—all these are examples of human resources which many infant schools would welcome. But not all infant schools need help to the same extent. The difficult decisions about allocating resources between schools have to be made by advisory and administrative staff. Evidence about the school's needs from a distribution of profile scores (Use 3) should clearly not be the only basis on which decisions should rest. But it is one extra piece of evidence to use.

The opportunity to predict individual attainment which Use 5 (p. 21) suggests is perhaps of more relevance to the local authority research worker. There is of course no reason why this approach should not be followed within the infant school, but it is not likely to be of as much interest to the majority of infant school teachers as some of the other uses.

Helping language development

The programme development unit was responsible for producing material for use in schools. Inevitably this unit relied more heavily on the research unit than did the Identification Techniques Unit. It therefore started its work some time after the rest of the project and finished a little out of phase too. Chapter 6 discusses the way in which this particular part of the project operated. It is worth noting again that from a fairly early stage in the project, it was decided not to attempt to develop the structured kind of programme which many American projects have preferred. It was felt that this approach would be alien to the tradition and the sentiment of the British infant school and so this unit was set the task of producing a guidebook or handbook, supported by examples of teaching games and materials, rather than a book of structured exercises. But this does not preclude the user developing her own set of structured language activities, designed with individual children in mind. The short discussion on pages 73 to 76 outlines the philosophy behind the use of the materials.

The programme was developed with the aid of groups of teachers who were largely concerned with children in the first year of their infant school experience, growing up in deprived areas. This gives the programme its flavour and sets its direction. But it would of course be wrong to suggest that the ideas in the handbook should be used exclusively with this age group or exclusively with children in this kind of area. This would be contrary to the philosophy of individual need on which the project has been based. The materials are of use for any child whose language usage is limited, irrespective of the sector of the education system. For example some teachers of nursery school children may find some ideas helpful. At the other extreme, some teachers of much older educationally subnormal children may also find some helpful ideas in the materials. So the programme can be of use with children of very different age groups from that for which it was primarily designed. The programme is not tied to any particular theory of language acquisition, as Chapter 6 indicates, and suggestions for using the ideas and activities in the classroom appear in the handbook itself.

The current interest in the language and its growth (Department of Education and Science, 1975) makes one realize how much our attitude towards language in schools has changed. The author remembers meeting with a group of infant school teachers in 1967, in the early days of the project and asking what activities they were using to foster the language development of their children. At that time, ten years ago, the main reaction was surprise at such a question being asked. Today, when the need for developing children's language rather than concentrating on reading and number development is much more widely accepted, the response would be very different.

Research findings

In much of this overview, the research work of the project has been seen as underpinning the work of the development units. An example of this is found in Chapter 5 which comments on the wide range of language skills found in children in working-class families. This helped to confirm the need for constructing assessment devices which included a measure of language skills and on the other hand a programme for teaching which again emphasized language. But as well as supporting the work of the development units, the research units (Unit for the Study of Emotional Development and Response to Schooling and the Welsh Language Unit) have made contributions to the understanding of child development at the infant school stage which are important in their own right. It is not easy to decide which of the different findings should be stressed in this final chapter. But in this section an attempt is made to indicate two or three findings which may be of particular interest to the work of the infant school teacher.

At a time when resources for extending the provision of nursery classes and schools are limited, the findings reported in 'Just Before School' (Chazan *et al*., 1971) may be helpful for example. They indicate the wide variation in the preparation for school which children are given. They offer the infant teacher some indication of the range of skills and attitudes in young children entering school from homes where parents have treated the question of school entry from very different points of view. The study itself, which was one of the earliest publications of the project, draws attention to the educational implications that follow from the findings.

It was not unexpected to find a significant gap in the language skills existing on average between children from advantaged home backgrounds and deprived home backgrounds. But the finding that this gap does not seem to widen across the three-year period of infant education is interesting. As Chapter 5 (p. 62) states, this is contrary to other work, notably in the U.S.A., where the cumulative effect of deprivation, especially in relation to language skills, has been widely regarded as a basic feature of child development in deprived areas. This piece of work needs replication, but it should not be surprising to find differences of this sort between the effects of deprivation in the U.S.A. and in this country. There are major differences in culture and in education which would lead one to be careful before importing an unmodified transatlantic concept of compensatory education. It was this line of argument which first led to the view that research into the nature of child development in deprived areas in England and Wales should be a necessary component of this project, which should not rely solely on theoretical findings derived from work in the U.S.A. Those readers with a special interest in the work of this intensive study will find it reported in Chazan et al. (1977). This finding can also be seen to support the view that in at least one critical area—language development—the British infant school succeeds in 'holding the gap' between deprived and advantaged children. It offers the hope that in our system the problem of trying to narrow the gap may be an easier one to solve than in the case of the U.S.A. It is tempting to speculate on the reasons for this. But in resisting that temptation, one cannot help observing that this finding can be seen as strengthening the view that the infant school may well prove to be the key point for successful intervention. The educational philosophy and approach of the infant school need refining, but not replacing.

Another point worth mentioning is the work of the research units on some of the characteristic features of behaviour problems in children of infant school age. Undesirable behaviour is a very difficult concept to delineate with precision: hence the percentage estimates given in any enquiry cannot be regarded as invariant. Nevertheless the view in Chapter 4 (p. 40) that the class teachers of the enquiry reported that just under a quarter of the children entering infant schools showed problems of behaviour and that just under a seventh needed attention for this reason, makes one think again about the need for specialists in the infant school whose concern would be the problems of emotional and social adjustment at the time children enter the school system. Readers interested in this part of the project's work will find it reported in Volumes I and II of Studies of Infant School Children (Chazan *et al.*, 1976, 1977).

The Welsh Language Study does not present a very encouraging picture of the development of the Welsh Language in schools which teach through the medium of Welsh. The sample of schools was of course a small one. But Chapter 7 (p. 94) draws attention to the extreme difficulty of the teachers' task in these schools. Although this was not the main objective of this enquiry, there seems to be a case for investigating the special problems of the teacher of infant children in the Welsh language medium schools. Again the findings suggest the need for treating children as individuals, rather than in groups. If bilingual children with varying language facility in the two languages are to be given a fair educational chance, then the resources needed for this must be made available. Readers interested in the findings of the bilingual side of the project's work will find it reported in Lloyd (1977).

Finally, many readers may feel that the emphasis so far placed on language and behaviour reflects a neglect of the traditional infant school objectives of reading and number work. This is not so. The development of these skills in infant school children and the relationship of home background to facilities in these skills is reported in Chazan *et al.* (1976, 1977).

The work of the identification techniques unit also led to the publication of a small longitudinal study of the development of early reading skills, 'Aspects of Early Reading Growth' (Davies and Williams, 1974). Readers with an interest in findings related to reading and number growth in the infant school are advised to turn to these two publications.

CONCLUSION

To write a conclusion to a chapter which is an overview of a book which is itself a short report of a major project is to invite oversimplification. What follows may be more in the nature of a postcript than a conclusion.

To this writer, the message that comes through from the work of the project is above all a message of the great differences that exist among the children who enter our infant schools. There are differences of preparation, of attitude, of home support, of behaviour, of language skills, of thinking processes—the list is endless and in every case the range is wide. To categorize their schools as 'deprived' or 'advantaged' is to label them too crudely and too unfairly. It is probably the all too obvious realization of this vast range of development that has led the infant schools to pioneer of necessity a teaching approach emphasizing the individual. Later sectors of the education system, where institutions are larger than the traditionally small infant school, and where pupils and students are older, may find teaching methods which rely more heavily on group work less inappropriate. In the infant school these methods are largely unsuitable.

This means that we have to acknowledge the stress placed on the infant school teacher through having to cope with the needs of a large number of very different children at a very vulnerable stage of their growth. The provision of educational aids is one step in this direction. A much greater step could be the provision of specialists who can carry out some of the tasks that this project suggests are needed.

These include conducting the screening of the needs of children entering the infant school, helping with the language development skills suggested through the use of this and other language development programmes, liaising with parents over the support and preparation that children need, and helping schools and parents and children over the management of some of the behaviour problems which arise at this stage of education and which have so far been relatively neglected.

Who should perform these tasks? Since they are in any case tasks which infant teachers currently have to carry out, though under great stress and inadequately, it could be argued that specially trained infant teachers would be best fitted for these roles. Others might argue that individuals who may not have experience of infant school teaching but who have expertise in areas like social work and child psychology would be at least as well fitted for the work.

But the final paragraph of a book is not the place to enter a debate about the preparation and training of specialists for work in infant schools. The project offers no evidence on this. But the need of large numbers of children, their families and their schools for extra assistance is plain to see for anyone reading the pages of the reports which the project has produced.

At the start of this chapter attention was drawn to the disparity between the research efforts directed at the secondary school and at the infant school. The presence in secondary schools of counsellors and remedial teachers and the existence of specialist employment services is other evidence of the attention that has also been paid to the needs of the adolescent and the school leaver. These provisions may be overstretched and inadequate, but they are generous indeed in comparison with those available for the infant school pupil and the school entrant. It is the contention of this overview that the case for similar resources, directed to the needs of children and parents at the point of entry to the infant school and during the first two or three years of education thereafter is at least as strong.

References

References

Publications etc. relating to the project are marked*

BARNES, J. H. (ed., 1975). *Educational Priority, Vol. 3: Evaluated Action in London and Birmingham.* London: HMSO

BARTLETT, E. J. (1972). Selecting preschool language programs. In CAZDEN, C. B. (ed.), *Language in Early Childhood Education.* Washington, D.C.: National Association for the Education of Young Children

BEREITER, C. and ENGELMANN, S. (1966). *Teaching Disadvantaged Children in the Preschool.* Engelwood Cliffs, N.J.: Prentice-Hall

BERNSTEIN, B. (1969). A critique of the concept of compensatory education. Paper given at the work conference of the Teachers' College, Columbia University, New York. (Published in BERNSTEIN, B. (1971). *Class, Codes and Control,* Vol. 1. London: Routledge and Kegan Paul)

BERNSTEIN, B.(1970). Education cannot compensate for society. *New Society,* 26th February, 1970

BERNSTEIN, B. (1971a). *Class, Codes and Control, Vol. 1: Theoretical Studies Towards a Sociology of Language.* London: Routledge and Kegan Paul

BERNSTEIN, B. (1971b) Social class, language and socialization. In ABRAMSON, A. S. *et al.* (Assoc. eds) *Current Trends in Linguistics,* Vol. 12. The Hague: Mouton Press. (Reprinted in BERNSTEIN, B. (1971). *Class, Codes and Control,* Vol. 1. London: Routledge and Kegan Paul)

BERNSTEIN, B. (1972). Personal communication to CAZDEN, C. B., cited in CAZDEN, C. B. (ed.), op. cit.

BISSELL, J. S. (1968). The cognitive effects of pre-school programs for disadvantaged children. In FROST, J. L. (ed.) *Early Childhood Education Rediscovered.* New York: Holt, Rinehart and Winston

BLANK, M. and SOLOMON, F. (1968). A tutorial language program to develop abstract thinking in socially disadvantaged preschool children. *Child Development,* 39, 379–389

BLANK, M. and SOLOMON, F. (1969). How shall the disadvantaged child be taught? *Child Development,* 40, 47–61

BOXALL, M. (1973). Nurture groups. *Concern* (National Children's Bureau), 12, 8–12

BRIMER, M. A. and DUNN, L. M. (1962). *English Picture Vocabulary Test I* and *Manual for the English Picture Vocabulary Tests* (covering Tests 1 and 2). Bristol: Educational Evaluation Enterprises

BRUNER, J. S. (1964). The course of cognitive growth. *Amer. Psychologist*, 20, 1007–1017

CAZDEN, C. B. (ed., 1972). *Language in Early Childhood Education*. Washington, D.C.: Nat. Ass. for the Education of Young Children

CENTRAL ADVISORY COUNCIL FOR EDUCATION, ENGLAND (1967). *Children and their Primary Schools (The Plowden Report)*. *Vol. 1: Children and their Primary Schools. Vol. 2: Research and Surveys*. London: HMSO

CENTRAL ADVISORY COUNCIL FOR EDUCATION, WALES (1967). *Primary Education in Wales (The Gittins Report)*. London: HMSO

*CHAZAN, M.(1968). Compensatory education: defining the problem. In *Compensatory Education: An Introduction*. Occasional Publication No. 1, Schools Council Research and Development Project in Compensatory Education. Department of Education, University College of Swansea

CHAZAN, M. (1969). Maladjustment and reading difficulties: recent research and experiment. *Rem. Educ.*, 4, 3, 119–123

CHAZAN, M. and COX, T. (1976). Language programmes for disadvantaged children. In WILLIAMS, P. and VARMA, V. P. (eds) *Piaget, Psychology and Education*. London: Hodder and Stoughton

*CHAZAN, M., COX, T., JACKSON, S. and LAING, A. F. (1977). *Studies of Infant School Children II: Deprivation and Development*. Oxford: Basil Blackwell (for Schools Council)

*CHAZAN, M. and JACKSON, S. (1971). Behaviour problems in the infant school. J. *Child Psychol. Psychiat.*, 12, 191–210

*CHAZAN, M. and JACKSON, S. (1974). Behaviour problems in the infant school: changes over two years. *J. Child Psychol. Psychiat.*, 15, 33–46

*CHAZAN, M., LAING, A. F., COX, T., JACKSON, S. and LLOYD, G. (1976). *Studies of Infant School Children I: Deprivation and School Progress*. Oxford: Basil Blackwell (for Schools Council)

*CHAZAN, M., LAING, A. F. and JACKSON, S. (1971). *Just Before School*. Oxford: Basil Blackwell

DAVIE, R., BUTLER, N. and GOLDSTEIN, H. (1972). *From Birth to Seven*. London: Longman

*DAVIES, P. and WILLIAMS, P. (1974). *Aspects of Early Reading Growth*. Oxford: Basil Blackwell (for Schools Council)

DEPARTMENT OF EDUCATION AND SCIENCE (1975). *A Language for Life* (*The Bullock Report*). London: HMSO

DEUTSCH, M. (1965). The role of social class in language development and cognition. *Amer. J. Orthopsychiat.*, 35, 78–88. (Reprinted in PASSOW, A. H., GOLDBERG, M. and TANNENBAUM, A. J. (eds) (1967). *Education of the Disadvantaged: A Book of Readings.* New York: Holt, Rinehart and Winston)

DEUTSCH, M. and BROWN, B. (1964). Social influences in Negro–White intelligence differences. *J. Soc. Issues*, 20, 2, 24–35

DOUGLAS, J. W. B. (1964). *The Home and the School.* London: MacGibbon and Kee

*DOWNES, G. (1978). *Language Development and the Disadvantaged Child.* Edinburgh: Holmes-McDougall (for Schools Council)

DUNN, L. M. and SMITH, L. O. (1964). *Peabody Language Development Kit.* Nashville, Tennessee: Insitute for Mental Retardation and Intellectual Development, George Peabody College for Teachers

*EVANS, R. (1973). *The Development and Evaluation of Some Techniques Used to Predict Educational Handicap in the Primary School.* Unpublished Ph.D. thesis, University of Wales (Swansea)

*EVANS, R. (1978). *Swansea Evaluation Profile for School Entrants: Technical Manual.* Included in the Swansea Evaluation Profile Kit; available for research applications only. Windsor: NFER Publishing Co. (for the Schools Council).

The longer preliminary version, entitled 'Early Technical Manual', is available for consultation by visitors to the Schools Council (Project Information Centre) or to the National Foundation for Educational Research (Library), or on loan from the NFER library

* EVANS, R., DAVIES, P., FERGUSON, N. and WILLIAMS, P. (1978). *Swansea Evaluation Profile for School Entrants*: Handbook. Included in the Swansea Evaluation Profile Kit; available for research applications only. Windsor: NFER Publishing Co. (for the Schools Council)

* EVANS, R. and FERGUSON, N. (1974). Screening school entrants. *Journal of the Association of Educational Psychologists*, 3, 6, 2–9

EYSENCK, H. J. (1969). The rise of the mediocracy. In COX, C. B. and DYSON, A. E. (eds), *Black Paper Two.* London: Critical Quarterly Society

* FERGUSON, N. (1972). *The Perceptual, Motor and Language Skills of Infant*

School Entrants. Unpublished Ph.D. Thesis, University of Wales (Swansea)

*FERGUSON, N., DAVIES, P., EVANS, R. and WILLIAMS, P. (1971). The Plowden Report's recommendations for identifying children in need of extra help. *Educ. Res.*, 13, 3, 210–213

*FERGUSON, N. and WILLIAMS, P. (1969). The identification of children needing compensatory education. In *Children at Risk*. Occasional Publication No. 2., Schools Council Research and Development Project in Compensatory Education. Department of Education, University College of Swansea

FRASER, E. (1959). *Home Environment and the School*. London: University of London Press

GAHAGAN, D. M. and GAHAGAN, G. A. (1970). *Talk Reform*. London: Routledge and Kegan Paul

GARDNER, D. E. M. (1950). *Testing Results in the Infant School*. London: Methuen

HALLIDAY, M. A. K. (1969). Relevant models of language. *Educ. Rev.*, 22, 26–37

HALSEY, A. J. (ed., 1972). *Educational Priority, Vol. 1: E.P.A. Problems and Policies*. London: HMSO

HAWKRIDGE, D. G., CHALUPSKY, A. B. and ROBERTS, A. O. H. (1968). *A Study of Selected Exploratory Programs for the Education of Disadvantaged Children*. U.S. Office of Education final report, project 089013

JENSEN, A. R. (1967). The culturally disadvantaged: psychological and educational aspects. *Educ. Res.*, 10, 4–20

JENSEN, A. R. (1971). Do schools cheat minority children? *Educ. Res.*, 14, 3–28

LABOV, W. (1970). The logic of non-standard English. In WILLIAMS, F. (ed.) *Language and Poverty*. Chicago: Markham Pub. Co.

LITTLE, A. and SMITH, G. A. N. (1971). *Strategies of Compensation: a Review of Educational Projects for the Disadvantaged in the United States*. Paris: Centre for Educational Research and Innovation. Organization for Economic Co-operation and Development

LLOYD, G. (1977). *Studies of Infant School Children, III—Deprivation and the Bilingual Child*. Oxford: Basil Blackwell (for Schools Council)

LURIA, A. R. (1961). *The Role of Speech in the Regulation of Normal and Abnormal Behaviour*. New York: Liveright

MCCARTHY, D. (1954). Language development in Children. In CAR-

MICHAEL. L. (ed.) *Manual of Child Psychology (2nd ed.)*. New York: Wiley

MORRISON, C. M. (ed., 1974). *Educational Priority, Vol. 5: EPA—a Scottish Study*. Edinburgh: HMSO

NEWTON, M. R. and BROWN, R. D. (1967). A Preventive Approach to Developmental Problems in School Children. Chapter 21 in BOWER, E. M. and HOLLISTER, W. G. (eds), *Behavioral Science Frontiers in Education*. New York: Wiley

PAGE, E. P. (1972). Miracle in Milwaukee: raising the IQ. *Phi Delta Kappan*, 1(10): 8–10, 15–16

PAYNE, J. (1974). *Educational Priority, Vol. 2: E.P.A. Surveys and Statistics*. London: HMSO

PHILLIPS, C. J., WILSON, H. and HERBERT, G. W. (1972). *Child Development Study (Birmingham 1968–71), Part I*. School of Education, University of Birmingham

PRINGLE, M. L. K., BUTLER, N. R., and DAVIE, R. (1966). *11,000 Seven-year-olds*. London: Longman

QUIGLEY, H. (1971). Nursery teachers' reactions to the Peabody Language Development Kit. *Brit. J. Educ. Psychol.*, 41, 2, 155-162

RUTTER, M. (1967). A children's behaviour questionnaire for completion by teachers: preliminary findings. *J. Child Psychol. Psychiat.*, 8, 1–11

SCHAEFER, E. S. (unpublished). *Classroom Behaviour Inventory*. Washington, D.C.: National Institute of Mental Health

SCHIFF, S. K. and KELLAM, S. G. (1967). A community-wide mental health program of prevention and early treatment in first grade. *Psychiatric Research Report* 21, American Psychiatric Research Report 21

SCHOOLS COUNCIL (1970). *Cross'd with Adversity: the Education of Socially Disadvantaged Children in Secondary Schools*. London: Evans/Methuen Educational

SHEPHERD, M., OPPENHEIM, B. and MITCHELL, S. (1971). *Childhood Behaviour and Mental Health*. London: HMSO

SMITH, G. (1975). *Educational Priority, Vol. 4: The West Riding. E.P.A.* London: HMSO

STOTT, D. H. (1966). *The Social Adjustment of Children (Manual to the British Social Adjustment Guides, 3rd edition)*. University of London Press

THOMAS, V. (1973). Children's use of language in the nursery school. *Educ. Res.*, 15, 209–216

TOUGH, J. (1971). Some differences in the use of language between two groups of three-year-old children. *Paper given to BPS (Education Section) Annual Conference*

TOUGH, J. (1973). The language of young children: the implications for the education of the young disadvantaged child. In CHAZAN, M. (ed.) *Education in the Early Years*. Faculty of Education, University College of Swansea and Aberfan Disaster Fund

TOUGH, J. (1977a). *The Development of Meaning*. London: Allen and Unwin

TOUGH, J. (1977b). *Talking and Learning: a Guide to Fostering Communication Skills in Nursery and Infant Schools*. London: Ward Lock Educational and Drake Associates

VYGOTSKY, L. V. (1962). *Thought and Language*. Cambridge, Mass.: MIT Press

WESTMAN, J. C., RICE, D. L. and BERMANN, E. (1967). Nursery school behaviour and later school adjustment. *Amer. J. Orthopsychiat.*, 3, 7, 4, 725–731

WILLIAMS, H. L. (1973). Compensatory Education in the nursery school. In CHAZAN, M. (ed.), *Compensatory Education*. London: Butterworths

*WILLIAMS, P. (1973). The Schools Council Research and Development Project in Compensatory Education. In CHAZAN, M. (ed.), *Compensatory Education*. London: Butterworths

*WILLIAMS P., CONGDON, P., HOLDER, M, and SIMS, N. (1971). *Swansea Test of Phonic Skills*. Oxford: Basil Blackwell

WOODHEAD, M. (ed., 1977). *An Experiment in Nursery Education*. Slough: NFER

Appendix

Appendix

Publications etc. relating to the project not listed above among references

CHAZAN, M. (1970). Cultural deprivation and reading readiness. In CHAZAN, M. (ed.), *Reading Readiness*. University College of Swansea Faculty of Education

CHAZAN, M. (1970). Difficulties of disadvantaged children. *Teacher in Wales*, 2, 3, 16–17

CHAZAN, M. (1971). Compensatory programmes for disadvantaged children. Cheshire: *Report of First National Conference of the Joint Council for the Education of Handicapped Children*, 76–81

CHAZAN, M. (1972). Compensatory education in the infant school. In HERMELIN, R. (ed.), *Teaching the Handicapped Child*. London: College of Special Education

CHAZAN, M. (1973). Disadvantage and nursery schooling. *Spec. Educ.*, 62, 3, 19–23

CHAZAN, M. and DOWNES G. (eds, 1971) *Compensatory Education and the New Media*. Occasional Publication No. 3, Schools Council Research Project in Compensatory Education. University College of Swansea, Department of Education

CHAZAN, M. and WILLIAMS, P. (1969). The Deprived and the Disadvantaged. *Dialogue* (Schools Council newsletter), 2, 12

COX, T. (1972). Study of the effects of cultural deprivation on aspects of children's development and school progress. *BPS Bull.*, 25, 65–66 (summary of paper read to annual meeting of BPS Education Section)

COX, T. (1973). *An enquiry into the association between cultural and material deprivation in the home background and aspects of infant school children's development*. Unpublished Ph.D. thesis, University of Wales

COX, T. and WAITE, C. A. (eds, 1970). *Teaching Disadvantaged Children in the Infant School*. Schools Council Research and Development Project in Compensatory Education and University College of Swansea Faculty of Education (out of print).

EVANS, R. (1973). The identification of children 'at risk' of educational handicap. *Urban Education*, 8, 1, 75–96

EVANS, R., DAVIES, P., FERGUSON, N. and WILLIAMS, P. (1975). The reliability of the Draw-a-Man test. *Educ. Res*, 18, 1, 32–36

FERGUSON, N. (1975). Pictographs and pre-reading skills. *Child Development*, 46, 786–789

LAING, A.(1971). The construction of an Infant School Amenities Index. *Brit. J. Educ. Psychol.*, 41, 1, 94–95

SCHOOLS COUNCIL RESEARCH AND DEVELOPMENT PROJECT IN COMPENSATORY EDUCATION (1970). *Infant School Amenities Index*

WILLIAMS, P., DAVIES, P., EVANS, R. and FERGUSON, N. (1970). Season of birth and cognitive development. *Nature*, 228, 5276, 1033–1036

Index

Index